THE RESIDENTIAL AGENT'S HANDBOOK
FOR COMMERCIAL REAL ESTATE

Reader Comments

"As a residential agent who is beginning to focus more on commercial properties, I found Brian's book to be the perfect guide. His vast knowledge and experience is a clear insight into the world of commercial real estate. With a huge list of resources and actionable steps outlining each chapter, this book is a sure-start way to success for any agent or broker looking to make the move into commercial real estate."

– Peter Garian, Residential Real Estate Agent

"Whether a residential agent is considering transitioning completely, or just trying to gain enough knowledge to be in the know for an occasional commercial transaction, this book delivers the goods. Readers can circumvent years of trial and error by tapping into Mr. Hennessey's knowledge of the industry's inside track. . . . This is not a one and done kind of book, but a valuable manual, to be referred to over and over, underlined and dog eared."

– Dina Novak, GRI, Realtor

"I have always wanted to incorporate commercial real estate into my residential business. To be honest, it has always seemed too daunting. After reading Brian's book and seeing how he breaks everything down in such a simple way, I am ready to tackle the next commercial referral that comes my way. No more giving away large chunks of money when I could put it in my pocket. I also like that I will become more valuable to my clients."

– Kathy Gardner, Realtor

"I've always wanted to have a friend in commercial real estate. Someone who will encourage me to start selling commercial properties, give helpful advice, and point me in the right direction. This is exactly what this book has done for me. I feel really empowered!"

– Mila Orgiyvsky, Residential Real Estate Agent

"I highly recommend this book to anyone who is on the fence about venturing into commercial real estate. Brian does an impressive job of not only applying his 30 years of expertise and experience, but really outlining the process in a clear concise manor and providing action items at the end of each chapter. This book is a truly an invaluable guide to anyone who is even remotely looking to venture into commercial real estate or simply wants to learn more about the industry."

– Angela Forgo, Residential Real Estate Agent

THE RESIDENTIAL AGENT'S HANDBOOK FOR COMMERCIAL REAL ESTATE

- ‣ NO-STRESS TRANSITION INTO COMMERCIAL REAL ESTATE TRANSACTIONS
- ‣ INCREASE YOUR EARNING POWER
- ‣ INCLUDES ESSENTIAL LETTER AGREEMENTS, SALE & LEASE FORMULAS, AND ACCESS TO COMMERCIAL FORMS

BY BRIAN HENNESSEY

Author of *The How to Add Value Handbook for Commercial Real Estate* and *The Due Diligence Handbook for Commercial Real Estate*

Printed in the United States of America
First Printing, 2018

ISBN-10: 0-9986163-3-9
ISBN-13: 978-0-9986163-3-9

YAJNA
PUBLICATIONS

Printed by Yajna Publications

Interior book design by Michelle M. White

Contents

Introduction

I have been in the commercial real estate industry for over 30 years. However, I started out in real estate on the residential end of the business. I never really became excited about listing and selling homes. I felt as though I was always working. Nights and weekends were spent fielding calls and negotiating transactions.

In the office where I worked, there were a couple of brokers who focused on commercial real estate. I would sometimes stop by to speak with them and asked them questions about commercial real estate transactions and commercial properties I had seen that perhaps I could work on with them. Their response was: "You are either in residential or commercial real estate, not both." That was just the way it was perceived back then.

In today's commercial real estate world, we see many real estate agents who work both residential and commercial real estate transactions. I believe the reason for this is that the Internet has leveled the playing field for real estate agents. They can now work for offices who offer them higher commission splits or even 100% of the commission and act as either residential or commercial brokerage firms. For example, RE/MAX, Keller Williams, and other firms offer agents maximum flexibility to work on their own.

This has led many residential brokers to start working in the commercial real estate end of the business. They can easily place a listing on a commercial real estate listing website alongside other commercial real estate brokerage firms, to offer their commercial listings and compete with them directly. This has become more acceptable, both from the principal and commercial brokerage side of the industry. It is no longer an anomaly.

I have met many agents who work both residential and commercial real estate quite successfully. Many of them are knowledgeable and are able to service their clients with a high degree of skill. I have also met residential agents who were marketing commercial listings with little or no knowledge of commercial real estate. I believe those agents are doing a disservice to their clients. Like any other business, you need to put forth the time and effort to acquire skills that will help you to succeed and provide the best service you are capable of. Those who do so are able to make a nice living for themselves while servicing their clients in a professional manner.

I wrote this handbook to help those residential real estate agents who wish to explore or get better at serving their clients in commercial real estate. Even though it was many years ago since I made the transition, I believe that I understand how someone can cross over, and I can help them to do it successfully.

In this book, I will offer you numerous ways to get started while you are doing residential real estate as well as helpful information that will help you to cross over entirely to the commercial real estate brokerage side of the industry. I will explain the various genres of commercial real estate and the benefits and challenges of each. I will also offer you tips and strategies on how to start generating income quickly, including examples of how leasing and investment sales can work.

I will present stories of residential agents who work commercial transactions and those who have learned the ins and outs of straddling the business. I also include a list of resources that will help you to build your knowledge base in commercial real estate.

I will be recommending books and other resources throughout this handbook, as well as a list of resources at the back of the book. Be sure to take advantage of these learning materials in order to expedite building your knowledge base in commercial real estate. If you do, it will pay off handsomely and get you up to speed much quicker.

More residential real estate agents are working commercial real estate transactions than ever before. They are reaping the financial benefits by being able to help their clients with all their real estate needs. It has never been easier than it is today. If you have been thinking about or have been involved with helping your clients with commercial real estate transactions, then you know it can be lucrative. This book will help you to take your knowledge and skill set to the next level in working on the commercial real estate side of the business.

Before we get started, I want to give you this quote by Tony Robbins:

> *"There are always two businesses you've got to manage, there's the business you're in, and the business you're becoming. If you just manage the business you're in, you're going to get knocked out by a new technology or new competition. But if you're constantly managing those two businesses, you won't have to quit or pivot, because you're always doing something to innovate, or to change, or to improve."*

The real estate brokerage industry is changing rapidly, and five years from now, it will not look anything like it does today.

So, let's get started on building your new skill set and knowledge base in commercial real estate to help you create a new revenue stream.

Brian Hennessey
Author of the #1 Best Seller *The Due Diligence Handbook for Commercial Real Estate* and *The How to Add Value Handbook for Commercial Estate*. Also, the instructor of "The Due Diligence Video Course for Commercial Real Estate" at impactcoachingsystems.com/courses.

CHAPTER 1

Why Consider Doing Commercial Real Estate Transactions as an Agent?

"We gain strength, and courage, and confidence by each experience in which we really stop to look fear in the face... we must do that which we think we cannot."
- Eleanor Roosevelt

The benefits of working commercial real estate

Having been in the commercial real estate industry for over 30 years, the one trend that stands out most is the amount of residential real estate agents who are now involved in commercial real estate transactions.

I believe this has to do with the fact that it is easier than ever for real estate agents to do both residential and commercial transactions. The internet has leveled the playing field not only for the real estate industry but for most industries out there. There are brokerage firms out there such as RE/MAX and Keller Williams that have both commercial real estate agents and residential agents that allows them to easily work both sides.

Traditionally, the commercial real estate industry did not have a multiple listing service like the ones used in residential real estate. Once CoStar and LoopNet came along, the commercial real estate industry had its version of a multiple listing service. Today, you will see many residential agents who have their commercial listings listed on LoopNet.

The interesting part is that many residential agents are asked by their clients if they also handle commercial real estate.

However, I can count the number of times I've been asked by commercial clients if I handle residential real estate on my right hand and have fingers left over. My sister, who is a successful residential real estate agent, has handled a number of commercial transactions for her clients. She has called me at various times asking about specifics on commercial properties. She has transitioned and worked these transactions successfully while doing her residential real estate business.

I regularly conduct seminars on commercial real estate at various brokerage offices and boards of realtors where there are a number of residential real estate agents looking to increase their knowledge of commercial real estate. Many of them come up to talk to me during the breaks about how they work their commercial real estate transactions. Some of them only work multifamily residential while others work all sides of the commercial end of the business.

I am convinced that residential real estate agents are more open to working commercial transactions than ever before. I give a seminar every year at our local Board of Realtors. I was told that their largest seminar attendance is the one given to real estate agents who are looking to learn more about commercial real estate transactions and how to win more of those in their business.

Myths and Facts

- **Myth number one:** Real estate agents can only work residential or commercial real estate, not both.

  Fact: As a licensed agent, you can work both commercial and residential.

- **Myth number two:** Most principals will only want to work with an agent who does one or the other.

  Fact: Many principals do not delineate real estate roles when it comes to residential and commercial, especially coming from the residential side.

- **Myth number three:** Commercial real estate transactions are too complex for most residential real estate agents.

  Fact: There are many commercial transactions that are simple. However, there are differences, and you do want to be aware of those, so you don't involve yourself or your client in potential litigation or financial problems.

- **Myth number four:** It takes too much time to learn how to do both residential and commercial real estate transactions.

  Fact: It does take time to learn the commercial side of the business, but you can do it incrementally like anything else you're trying to learn. It's not rocket science.

- **Myth number five:** I will hurt my reputation as a residential agent if I do commercial transactions as well.

  Fact: I've spoken with many residential agents who believe that it has had no deleterious effect on their residential business.

- **Myth number six:** Commercial real estate agents will not take me seriously when inquiring about commercial properties.

  Fact: There are always people out there who are "elitists" and think more of themselves because you're not a commercial agent. However, most are respectful and helpful. The more knowledgeable and professional you are when speaking to them, the easier it will be for them to take your inquiry seriously. It is more commonplace than ever for residential agents to get involved on the commercial side of the business.

- **Myth number seven:** You must learn financial analysis before working commercial real estate.

  Fact: If you are planning on working investment property sales it would be beneficial, and I would suggest, studying and taking some courses to help you understand how the numbers work. You'll then be in a much better position to help your clients and yourself.

- **Myth number eight:** It is too difficult to convince clients that I can help them with their commercial real estate needs.

  Fact: If you sound like you know what you're talking about, it won't be all that hard. You need to start building your knowledge base, which won't be too difficult if you work at it regularly.

- **Myth number nine:** You must learn all the various specialties in commercial real estate before working on commercial transactions.

  Fact: You can learn the various specialties as you decide to work on several types of transactions. You may decide you don't have an interest in learning a specific type of commercial, such as leasing or industrial, office or retail.

- **Myth number ten:** The commissions are much larger on commercial transactions.

  Fact: It's true that the dollar size of some of the transactions can get quite large. Generally speaking, the commission percentage drops considerably once the transactions get above $8M-$10M on sales of properties. It can vary as much as 3%-4% of the purchase price, depending upon where it is and what type of product, the demand, supply, etc. Above that amount, it's typical to see 1%-2% of the purchase price.

The Benefits

By learning how to crossover from residential real estate to the commercial real estate side of the business, you will afford yourself another opportunity to make more money by helping your clients. If you have already helped your clients on the residential side, then they already like and trust you. If you have discovered that they have a need on the commercial real estate side, then all you have to do is demonstrate that you have the knowledge to help them make an informed and intelligent decision.

Having already built trust with your client is a huge step forward. Now, you must help them to take the necessary steps in reaching their objectives with their commercial real estate needs.

Having another opportunity to create income gives you more versatility. When presented with opportunities to get involved with a commercial real estate transaction, you will be ready to take advantage.

The Challenges

Once you have made the decision to start working on the commercial real estate side of the business, it is easy to become intimidated. Not knowing what to ask, what the principal factors are, and just not being familiar will make you feel hesitant to inquire about commercial properties. Just remember, everybody starts out from the same place. As you acquire new knowledge and skill sets, you will begin to feel more comfortable when talking to others about it.

My suggestion is to start getting yourself familiar with commercial real estate jargon and knowledge. There are numerous ways to do this, which are included in this book.

Remember, everything seems difficult at first. I remember that when I first started out in the commercial real estate business, I had very little knowledge. In fact, back then, there weren't as many resources as there are our today to learn the business. Today, you can get up to speed on just about any subject quickly and easily.

There are books, audiobooks, podcasts, video courses, community college extension courses, and webinars. If you want to get a head start, go on Amazon.com and order the top five commercial real estate books or any of the ones you believe will help you get started. Also, go on Audible.com and check out the variety of audiobooks they have available on commercial real estate. I have two audiobooks on there: *The Due Diligence Handbook for*

Commercial Real Estate and *The How to Add Value Handbook for Commercial Real Estate.* Both will give you a good foundation of knowledge to get started.

Action Items

➠ Make the decision and commitment to start building your knowledge and skill sets in commercial real estate
➠ Create a game plan and then implement your first steps in working in commercial real estate
➠ Put aside one hour a day to read or listen to audiobooks or podcasts about commercial real estate
➠ Enroll in an online course or video course that teaches you an aspect of commercial real estate

CHAPTER 2

Today's Real Estate World

"Security is mostly a superstition. It does not exist in nature, nor do the children of men as a whole experience it. Avoiding danger is no safer in the long run than outright exposure. Life is a daring adventure or nothing at all."
~ Helen Keller

Current trends in the commercial real estate brokerage industry

More people are interested in diversifying their investment portfolios with commercial real estate than ever before. The most popular commercial real estate genre is apartments; however, many investors look to industrial, retail and office properties as well.

Another very popular type of commercial real estate ownership are owner/user properties. These are properties that small to medium-size business owners use for their own purposes to run their businesses in. We will talk about this in more detail a little bit later.

Many residential agents are taking an interest in commercial real estate. There are many reasons that this may be a trend in residential real estate offices. As this happens more frequently, residential agents see their associates tapping into an additional income stream and start doing the same.

How this affects both residential and commercial real estate agents

Commercial agents are quickly becoming used to the idea that there are residential agents ready, willing, and able to cross-over and work both sides of the real estate world. As real estate agents become more knowledgeable and comfortable working commercial real estate transactions, they will start to work at larger, more complex transactions, depending upon the type and scope of the client's needs.

There are times when a residential agent may not have yet acquired the knowledge of the type of transaction their client needs help with and will better serve them by referring them to a commercial real estate agent who specializes in their particular need.

Some commercial real estate agents are willing to help guide a residential agent through a transaction that they may not be totally familiar with. However, if a commercial agent feels they are carrying more than their fair share of the work load in completing the transaction, they may ask for an adjustment on the commission split.

Many clients are open to residential agents doing both homes and commercial real estate

Your client's comfort level will depend upon several factors. Some of which are:

- How you as their agent approach their inquiry or need for assistance with commercial real estate, for instance, asking the proper questions and having the right responses that indicate that you are in fact knowledgeable and comfortable in discussing their commercial real estate needs.
- The size and scope of their needs and your experience in handling these types of transactions.
- How you demonstrate your knowledge, ability, and resources.

What the future is going to look like for real estate agents

It's difficult to say exactly what it will look like in the next 5 to 10 years. At some point there will be more disintermediation (removal of the agent) in the process for some real estate transaction types. The innovation and integration of blockchain technology, which is defined as "a digital database containing information (such as records of financial transactions) that can be simultaneously used and shared within a large decentralized, publicly accessible network". As artificial intelligence (AI) takes over more of the clerical, administrative and financial tasks it will speed up the process and remove the need for outside help and intermediaries to consummate transactions. This is inevitable for many industries such as insurance, financial agents, i.e. mortgage brokers, loan correspondents and many other "white collar" jobs.

Due to the proliferation of websites with information containing availabilities, sale and lease comparables, various metrics, history of the market and product, and other pertinent information, will collectively and definitely have an impact on how people conduct real estate transactions in the near future.

As buyers and sellers, and tenants and landlords become more accustomed to dealing directly with each other, the need for an intermediary will become less needed.

I liken it to the travel agency industry in which people would call up the travel agent to book their flights, hotel reservations, etc. Most all of that was replaced digitally mainly because they are easier tasks to perform by most individuals on their computers, tablets, or even mobile phones. By the way, we recently used a travel agent for our family summer vacation who came highly recommended. She was extremely helpful and knowledgeable. With her help and guidance we planned a memorable vacation for our family that we will always treasure.

There are some prognosticators who believe this will happen in real estate sooner rather than later. I am of the belief that there is still a need for agents to assist others in working out differences and deciphering the information in the marketplace. So, as long as there is a need for this, the role of the real estate agent is not going away anytime soon.

I do believe that agents will still be needed for the more 'complex' real estate transactions that require human interpretation and background experience for issues and questions that a computer will not be able to solve. The internet can answer questions and address issues and problems that are only as good as the questions presented, and even that is limited. For the time being anyway, computers will not be able to determine the answers that only professional expertise can.

How real estate agents can prepare now for the foreseeable future

One way you as a real estate agent can prepare for the foreseeable future is to be more diversified in the types of real estate transactions you can handle. I truly believe that if you are able to help others to make informed and intelligent decisions when buying, selling,or leasing investment real estate, you will always have a service that's in demand. You have to be able to add value to your clients and explain to them cogently and succinctly how you will do that for them. Keep adding to your knowledge base and skillset as long as you're in the business of helping others.

Some believe that they shouldn't handle more than one type of real estate genre. Although I've met many in my market, in Los Angeles, who do quite well diversifying their efforts. In some markets where the volume and velocity of transactions are much smaller, it can make tremendous sense to be able to have the flexibility to do various types of real estate transactions.

It is easier for a residential agent to crossover into both, now more than ever before. That is not the case for commercial real estate agents. As I mentioned previously, it is rare to find one who does mostly commercial real estate and occasionally sells homes. As a residential real estate agent, you may find after working on commercial real estate transactions that you enjoy the diversification and ability to work another real estate genre and increase your income. You will never know if you don't give it a try. Try to keep your mind open to learning a new aspect in your industry. You may be surprised how much you like it and enjoy the flexibility. Who knows, it may end up that you spend more time in commercial than residential or end up liking it so much you decide to go full-time in it.

CHAPTER 3

How to Get Started as a Commercial Real Estate Agent

"Strive not to be a success, but rather to be of value."
~ *Albert Einstein*

Building a Referral System

One way to start earning income with your clients in commercial real estate is by building a referral network for the various genres. This will not only start you earning income but also expose you to the different types of commercial property types and how they are handled.

When I first got into the commercial end of the business I had no idea what specialty I wanted to get into. A successful attorney friend of the family once gave me some good advice when I was a teenager when I asked him what type of law I should go into. He said, *"You don't pick the specialty; let the specialty pick you."* Meaning, see what you naturally gravitate towards once you've been exposed to the different types of specialties.

I tried working with different brokers in the office on the different types of real estate they were handling when first starting out in the commercial side. I eventually found I liked the office leasing and sales end of the business more than the others and decided to focus on it. I've spent the majority of my career in commercial real estate focused on office properties. However, I have worked on, brokered, managed, owned, and handled other types, so I have had experience with all the commercial genres over my career. They all have their positive and negative points and nuances. You'll have to figure out where you will thrive and what you enjoy focusing on.

Various ways to start earning income

You can start 'earning while learning' about commercial real estate transactions and values by referring business to other agents who work commercial. Typical referrals run anywhere from 10% to 25% of the commission earned, depending upon the transaction and how much you're involved in delivering the assignment or listing. If it's just passing along a name of someone who you met in passing or heard about then it will most likely be on the lower end of the scale. If it's someone who you have a good relationship with and they're basically going with your recommendation, then it should be at the higher end.

The commission referral will be based on the total sales price or total leasehold value if it's a lease. Be sure to clarify that it's on either the buy or sell side, or the landlord or tenant rep side that you'll be paid on.

ALWAYS get your agreement in writing. Even if it's just an email, although I recommend a letter or form agreement. If asked, "Don't you trust me?", tell them it's not a matter of trust but a "written confirmation of an understanding so that there is no misunderstanding later." If they're unwilling to confirm your understanding or sign an agreement with you, take that as a 'red flag' warning.

Start meeting commercial agents of the various specialties

I recommend that you start networking with commercial agents or other residential agents that do both. Begin gathering information on what types of properties they work on and if they would pay a referral fee should you have someone who may have a need that they can help you with. Once you start gathering information on the different commercial property types, you'll feel more comfortable discussing particulars about clients' needs.

The idea is to get to know the agents who work commercial properties and let them get to know you. Once they see you're becoming more knowledgeable and can converse with them in their language, (which isn't all that complex once you start learning the ropes), they will be more likely to want to transact and work collaboratively with you at higher splits and even split the fee earned with you. That would obviously depend upon the size and scope of the project, though.

Knowing and being known by the people who are working the commercial properties and transactions in your marketplace is the name of the game.

The best way to make yourself known is to call and introduce yourself. Obviously, it will be easier to do if you have a specific requirement and you are calling on one of their signs or listings. If you're calling up just to chat with them, it can be a bit awkward. You can always say you're gathering "preliminary information" for a "client" and would like to get the information on their listing. Ask them what other listings they have they can share with you. Be sure to let them know that you'll be getting back to them when you get "further down the road" with your "client." Most will be happy to accommodate you.

Another way I like to meet people is to connect with them on LinkedIn. Afterwards, give them a call and ask the receptionist to connect them if they don't answer direct. When the receptionist asks what's it regarding, say, "We're connected on LinkedIn." Most of the time, they will put you through. Then, when the person you're trying to reach gets on the line, tell them you're calling because you like to make your connections "real" on LinkedIn. You were wondering if there was a chance you could get together for coffee or just meet to discuss how you may be able to send business their way and vice versa. You'll be surprised at how many people will say yes.

Be patient with yourself

Remember, it takes time to get familiar with the various properties and transaction types in the commercial arena. Give yourself the time and patience required to lay the foundational steps, language and financial analysis needed for each property type. You will eventually get up to speed and feel like it's been a part of you since you've been in the business.

It's important to realize that it is always difficult when starting out. Everyone starts out from the same place at the beginning, with little to no knowledge. No one knows everything, so don't worry about not knowing things or not having all the answers.

Don't try to fake your way into commercial transactions

One thing I will admonish you about is to not try to fake it when asked about something you don't know. If you don't know something, just tell them you're not sure, but you'll get back to them with an answer once you find out more about it. People are much more receptive to that than hearing some false response that sounds like nonsense, or worse, they already have the answer to and now have heard you put your foot in your mouth. Believe me, everything else you say after that will be considered untrustworthy.

I once met an agent who said his client was interested in a small building I had listed and asked if they could tour it with me the next afternoon. I met them at the property and started asking some qualifying questions of the client. Their agent started speaking for his client and responded with some ridiculous answers that his client quickly corrected with an annoyed tone. After a few more misstated remarks the agent made, his client finally asked him in front of me if he had ever done any commercial transactions before. He said a couple of them, but not like this particular property type. His credibility was definitely not giving his client a comfort level he was looking for. We did not get the chance to work on the transaction together; I believe it was because his client moved on to another agent. He would have been better off not saying anything than trying to act as though he was knowledgeable.

Action Items

➠ Start building your network of commercial agents in your marketplace. You can do this by going to networking events and classes at your local board of realtors.

➠ Make it your business to meet as many commercial agents in your area as you can so that you get to know whom you can call for several types of properties, either for referrals or for a particular need once you get to know the business better.

CHAPTER 4

Start the Learning Process

"We become what we think about."
~ *Earl Nightingale*

Start learning about the various commercial real estate genres

To speak intelligently about the various genres of commercial real estate, you have to have some basic knowledge about each of them. There are four basic genres in the industry: multifamily, retail, office, and industrial. The most popular of all the genres is multifamily properties. That's because there are lots of them and they are the easiest investment properties to learn about and manage.

Eventually, you will find that you will have a propensity towards one or more of the genres. It may be multifamily properties, retail, or investments in general. If you do decide to just work investments, then you will need to learn about the various genres that you may be working with. Either way, you want to become an expert in one or more of the property types. That way you can speak cogently and intelligently with investors and sellers.

Finding a Mentor

I highly recommend you find yourself a mentor that can help you to learn more about the specialty you're interested in and about commercial real estate in general. This will save you years of trial and error learning. Finding a mentor is not all that difficult. However, I will give you some tips to make the process easier.

Once you identify someone that you think would be a good mentor, make certain you don't become one of those students who quickly becomes a nuisance. What I mean specifically is that you don't want to bombard them with questions and requests. Ask them if there is some way that you can be of help to them. Learn all you can about them so that you can know how you might be able to assist them with an organization they're involved with, a charity that they contribute to, or some other useful help you may be able to offer.

By the way, you can have more than one mentor. I have had different mentors for various aspects of my business and personal life. Most successful people are happy to share their knowledge and business experience with others who are open and teachable. I am extremely grateful to those mentors I have had in my life, who made a major difference and saved me from having to make a lot of mistakes in trial and error.

One way to identify potential mentors is to join organizations specific to the commercial real estate industry, such as Certified Commercial Investment Member (CCIM), which is a prestigious educational institution that offers courses in commercial real estate investments for real estate professionals and investors. Once you complete their course curriculum, you receive the CCIM designation, which is highly regarded in the commercial real estate industry. You can also join Building Owners and Managers Association (BOMA), Urban Land Institute (ULI), or Institute of Real Estate Management (IREM). These and other organizations offer excellent educational programs and have some of the top professionals in the industry who teach their members. If you are serious about becoming excellent as a commercial real estate professional, you will want to consider joining one of these highly regarded institutions.

The many ways to build your knowledge base in commercial real estate

Fortunately, for those just entering the commercial real estate industry, there are many different avenues and resources that allow you to build your knowledge foundation quickly and easily. When I first got into the business over 30 years ago most people basically had to go to their local college or universities for extension courses offered. I was fortunate enough to live close by UCLA in West Los Angeles. It offered numerous courses in commercial real estate, some of which were taught by prominent instructors and real estate attorneys. I took every commercial real estate course that it offered. Other than that, people were limited to a handful of books, some periodicals, and occasional seminars.

In today's world the Internet offers you a plethora of video courses, books, audiobooks, podcasts, ezines, webinars, and websites that host all sorts of useful information. If you are disciplined, you can get yourself up to speed in the commercial real estate industry in a brief period of time. However, you will need to be diligent and spend at least one hour per day studying all the various aspects in the industry. If you do, you can become an expert in the top 5% of the industry within three to five years. There is no reason that you can't make that happen unless you are unwilling to spend the necessary time and energy.

There's another way you can potentially speed up the learning process, if you want to go full time in commercial real estate. If you're just out of college or under 35 years old, you can look for a "runner position" for a senior broker who has been in the industry for several years and is looking for help in growing their business. Essentially, they will be looking for someone to research properties, prospect for sellers and investors, help put together marketing materials, follow up on business, and assist in many various factors in conducting the brokerage into the business. Depending upon the brokerage firm, the individual broker you will be working with, and whatever other specific requirements they may have of you, there is sometimes a monthly stipend or small monthly salary and a small percentage of any transactions that you help to complete. This can run anywhere from 5% to 20%. The other way, there are bonuses paid based on production at the end of the year. These "runnerships" can last anywhere from one year to three years. It can also blossom into a full-time partnership if the synergy is there with both parties and if they want to work it that way.

Some of the larger commercial real estate firms such as CBRE, JLL, Cushman & Wakefield, HFF, Marcus & Millichap, Avison Young, Colliers International, and others offer "runnerships." Many of these recruits come from summer internships who showed some promise and desire to get into the industry.

Make the commitment

If you are serious about learning the commercial real estate industry, then you will have to decide whether or not you're going to make the commitment to learn all you can about it. It's like anything else in life; if you "kind of" have an interest in it, then most likely, you're not going to get very far in building your knowledge base or earning income by doing commercial real estate transactions.

I can promise you this; if you do make the commitment and decide that you want to learn as much as possible, and you develop a program for yourself so that you are studying regularly, learning, and practicing your new skills, it can pay off handsomely for you.

I've met many people, including residential real estate agents, who said they were very interested in learning the commercial real estate business. When I asked them what they were doing to increase their knowledge or learn more about it, most of them told me that they were not doing anything about it. In other words, they didn't even have a plan. Put a plan together for yourself and make the commitment to study regularly and learn all you can. There are just too many ways for you to get started to make any excuses.

Action Items

⇒ Make a list of the ways that you enjoy learning new subjects. If it's video courses, look up the video courses available in commercial real estate. You can start by signing up for my course, *"The Due Diligence Video Course for Commercial Real Estate"* at: impactcoachingsystems.com/courses, which will give you an excellent foundation of knowledge for helping others, as well as yourself, to purchase real estate investments. **(Use the code: rahb25 at checkout for a 25% discount off the course prices. You can also get a certificate of completion and digital badge to use on LinkedIn or any other website where it's applicable by taking an exam.)**

⇒ If you like to listen to podcasts, then subscribe to one or more of the commercial real estate podcasts that are available.

⇒ If you have a community college or university nearby, check out their extension courses and see what they have available. You may be pleasantly surprised.

CHAPTER 5

The Various Commercial Real Estate Types

"Twenty years from now you will be more disappointed
by the things that you didn't do than by the ones
you did do, so throw off the bowlines,
sail away from safe harbor, catch the trade winds
in your sails. Explore, Dream, Discover."
~ *Mark Twain*

Apartments/Multifamily Properties

Just about every community has some multifamily residential properties located there. Many commercial real estate investors start out with owning multifamily properties and move later to other commercial real estate genres. The remarkable thing about multifamily properties is everybody needs a place to live. Depending upon the community you live in, there may be little or no competition. However, there are communities that have a multitude of apartment projects and not enough tenants to fill them. This could be due to an overbuilt environment or a major employer moving out of the area. No matter what the reason, if you're an investor you need to investigate why this is the case and if it makes sense to invest in multifamily properties in that area.

The good news is that for many of the major metropolitan areas and secondary markets, the demand for multifamily properties won't peak for a while. That means there is plenty of room for development and tenant demand for the foreseeable future.

If you're planning on helping others to invest in multifamily properties, you need to learn the ins and outs of the numbers, the market rents, the market trends, the vacancy factor, any extraneous factors that may affect the occupancy such as overbuilding or major employers moving out of the area, and a myriad of other factors that could affect multifamily investments.

There are numerous ways to start learning about multifamily property investments. I recommend getting yourself a few books on Amazon where there are many excellent books on the subject. One of my favorite books on multifamily properties is *The Complete Guide to Buying and Selling Apartment Buildings* by Steve Burges. He does an excellent job of explaining how to evaluate and investigate multifamily investments. He also speaks from experience as an investor and syndicator. He offers fitting examples and stories to illustrate the lessons he's learned, as well as valuable forms and checklists.

Another book I would highly recommend helping you become familiar with financial analysis of commercial real estate investments is *What Every Real Estate Investor Needs to Know About Cash Flow* by Frank Gallinelli. It is a terrific guide to understanding how numbers work when investing in commercial investment properties.

Once you learn these principles and formulas you will be miles ahead of your competition and be able to help yourself and others at a much higher level than most commercial real estate brokers and investors understand.

Office Properties

Office properties are the most complex of all the commercial real estate genres. This is because of the way leases are typically structured for most office properties. Typically, the way office leases work is the landlord will pay most or all the operating expenses of the property while the tenant pays a base rent on the prorated percentage of the square footage which they occupy. In a multitenant office building, there is generally a load factor attributed to the common areas such as the hallways, lobby area, restrooms, and other essential rooms, such as janitorial closets, less any vertical penetrations for stairwells and elevator shafts. For example, if 15% of the building is the equivalent of the common area square footage, and the tenant occupies 1000 sq. ft. of usable square footage (usf), then the 15% load factor will be added on to the 1000 sq. ft. for a rentable square footage (rsf) of 1150 (1000usf x 1.15 Load Factor= 1150rsf).

Building Owners and Managers Association (BOMA) has a standardized format for the measurement of commercial properties. I highly recommend getting a copy of it for future reference, so you can explain to others what the acceptable standards of measurement for each of the genres of commercial real estate are, such as office, industrial, or retail properties. Go to www.BOMA.org for more information.

If it is a single tenant office building, then the tenant will pay for the entire building square footage, and it will generally be on a triple net basis where the tenant pays for all the expenses plus their base rent.

One of the reasons that office properties and investments are the most complex is that the operating expenses of running the property are in the structuring of the leases. Let's say that, for example, there is an office building of 25,000 sq. ft., and the property costs the landlord $10 a square foot per year to operate the building. This would include property taxes, insurance, maintenance, janitorial services, utilities, repairs, landscape maintenance, and trash removal. That would equate to $250,000 per year of operating expenses.

Typically, office buildings are rented on a gross/full service basis, meaning the landlord will pay all the operating expenses. However, a tenant running 5000 sq. ft. (20% of the building) will be responsible for any increases of operating expenses over and above their base year, which is the calendar year or sometimes the first 12 months of occupancy of their lease term. The base year establishes the baseline operating expenses of the building.

For example, if the building costs $10 per square foot in operating expenses the first year of the lease term, and in the second-year, expenses go up 5%, or $.50 per square foot, then the tenant will pay their pro rata share of the increase in expenses, or 20% of the increase.

There are times when instead of a base year, the landlord will negotiate an "expense stop," which is a number estimated to be the operating expenses of the building.

If you are going to get involved with the negotiating leases for office buildings, you need to have a good understanding of how the leases work.

You will be paid on the total leasehold value of the lease executed by the tenant landlord. In most cities, that equates to a 4% to 6% commission, depending upon whether it is a full service or triple net lease.

Learn what you can about office leases by reading books or listening to webinars and seminars, then jump in and start the process by helping a client to negotiate a lease. A good place to start and learn the fundamentals would be with my book, *The How to Add Value Handbook for Commercial Real Estate*. In it, I have sample proposals and discuss how the various types of leases work and are structured. I also give you access on my website, www.impactcoachingsystems.com, under the Resources tab, where there are numerous lease samples and other valuable complimentary resources and forms that you can use in creating value for yourself and others.

Industrial

Industrial properties are more straightforward due to the fact that they are generally large boxes with little or no offices. The expenses are usually paid by the tenants, with the landlord being responsible for the exterior of the building, roof, and some other negotiated expenses of the property.

There are different factors to take into consideration when leasing industrial properties. For example, different tenants have different requirements for power, clear height needs within the building, loading docks, circulation on the property for trucks' ingress and egress, access to railroad spurs, drainage, and highway access, just to name a few.

The best way to familiarize yourself with industrial leases is to read through one so that you have a better understanding of how the leases work and the importance of the various provisions for both the landlord and the tenant.

Industrial landlords, depending upon the market, pay typically 2% to 5% of the total leasehold value as a commission.

Retail

Retail properties have their own set of issues and concerns that you need to be aware of if you plan on selling or leasing them. For example, if we're talking about small retail centers, you need to be aware of the tenant mix, parking availability and the impact that certain tenants may have upon it, access to and from the property, what and where the competition is and how it may affect the tenants of the property, and various other factors.

Generally, retail leases are on a triple net basis, meaning the tenant pays all or most of the operating expenses of the property on a pro rata share basis. There will be variations of how expenses are allocated, depending upon the market, competition, and other considerations. The pro rata share means that they will have a per square foot base rent, plus any common area maintenance expenses of the property (CAM charges).

As an agent, they will also be paid on the total leasehold value obligated by the tenant. This does not include CAM charges. Retail landlords are not generally going to be paying you the same rate as an office lease. However, depending upon the marketplace, you may get 3% to 5% of the total leasehold value by representing the tenant.

Action Items

➠ In order to make money leasing commercial properties, make yourself familiar with the various provisions in leases for the genres you want to work with.

➠ Start familiarizing yourself with the properties that are available for lease or for sale in this genre that you are interested in working on. Call on the brokers and ask to receive information on the property. If it's for lease, ask if they have a leasing flyer they can send you. If it's for sale, ask for a sale prospectus or offering memorandum.

➠ Don't be intimidated to jump in and start asking questions and collecting information on properties. The only way you're going to start working on the commercial side of the business is by jumping in with both feet. Remember, everybody starts out at the same place. There are plenty of resources available on the internet, so you can start familiarizing yourself with all the various commercial real estate genres.

CHAPTER 6

The Basics of Leasing Commercial Properties

"I am not a product of my circumstances.
I am a product of my decisions."
~ *Stephen Covey*

What You Need to Know

We touched briefly on some leasing aspects in the last chapter. If you want to learn how leases are negotiated, proposals are made and what the various lease forms and provisions look like, I highly recommend my book *The How to Add Value Handbook for Commercial Real Estate*. In it you'll find many examples and explanations of lease proposals. You can also see these and sample lease forms on my website at www.impactcoachingsystems.com under the Resources tab. I also share many of the lessons, tips, and strategies I've learned over the years and the expertise of others who are specialists in their genre.

In this chapter, I want to point out how you may get started in learning how to lease the various commercial properties. We'll assume that you have networked and introduced yourself to some of the commercial leasing brokers in your area.

How to Get Started in Leasing

Now, you have a requirement from a prospective tenant/client who is looking for a lease space in your market. You will have to do a survey of the available spaces that fit your client's criteria. Hopefully you'll have access to CoStar, LoopNet, or some other web-based listing directory to conduct your search (see more websites under Resources at the back of this book).

Another way is to drive around the area and look for lease signs on the properties that may fit your client's genre/requirements. Call the brokers handling those properties and collect the data necessary to find out whether it's a fit for your client. You will want to put the information on a tenant survey form or spreadsheet which will allow you to list out the various properties with their pertinent information for your client's review. You can find a tenant survey form on my website and a sample form at the back of this book, as well.

After you've collected all the data and put it on the form, set up a time to discuss it with your client to talk about the various properties, their pros and cons, and any other information that you'd like to share with them regarding the alternative spaces. Perhaps the listing brokers have furnished you with leasing brochures, floor plans, and other information.

My recommendation is you get an agreement signed by your client stating that they will work with you exclusively in their search for lease space. At the very least, they need to understand that you will only be paid for your time and expertise and it's very important that they work with you exclusively and not call on many brokers to help them with their lease space requirement. If you don't, you run the chance of them calling around on their own and going direct to the buildings' listing broker. Then, you will be out of the picture and will have worked for free. I have a sample 'Exclusive Right to Represent' letter agreement on my website under the Resources tab and at the back of this book that you can use on your letterhead and modify according to your needs. If you don't protect yourself, then you are just throwing the dice and hoping it all works out, which is not a good plan.

Once you have determined which properties work best for your client's needs, then you can set up a tour to go out and look at the properties with your client. After that, you'll be in a better position to determine which ones will work best for them. Then, you will generate a lease proposal for each of those properties your client has chosen to negotiate with.

Here is a Sample Lease Proposal to give you an idea of what information is included and how it outlines the salient terms under which a lease could be drawn. Each type of commercial space will have its variations and nuances of requirements and specific needs. These leases can vary dramatically in terms of length of lease term, rental rate structure, landlord contribution, security requirements from tenant, access, and utilities, just to name a few. This sample lease proposal is for an office lease:

SAMPLE LEASE PROPOSAL

February 29, 20__

Sent via e-mail to: .com
Mr. Tenant Rep Broker
Senior Vice President
Big Time Commercial Real Estate
12345 Main St.
Major Metro, CA 91436

Re: Lease Proposal – Tenant's Name

Dear _____:

Thank you for touring your client, Major Corp, Inc., through our building. On behalf of _____ ("Landlord"), I have been authorized to present to (Tenant's Name) ("Tenant") the following proposal to lease office space at 12345 Main Street, Your Town, Your State ("Building"). If the following terms and conditions meet with your approval, please sign below and we will proceed to have a lease document drafted to incorporate such terms and conditions.

BUILDING/ PREMISES:	Approximately half of the building located at 12345 Main Street, Your Town, Your State (the "Building"), consisting of approximately 10,000 usable square feet (the "Premises"), subject to final space planning. The common area load factor and RSF shall be determined upon completion of final space planning. Tenant shall provide the initial space plan for Landlord's review.
LEASE TERM:	The term of the Lease shall be eight (8) years and shall commence upon the later of (i) substantial completion of the Tenant Improvements to be performed by the Landlord in the Premises ("Commencement Date") or (ii) November 1, 2__.
MONTHLY BASIC RENTAL:	The Monthly Basic Rental during the initial Lease Term shall be as follows:

Month   Monthly Basic Rent per RSF

1–12   *$3.10, Net of utilities &
          janitorial for the premises

*The Monthly Basic Rent shall be increased by three percent (3%) per annum thereafter.

TENANT IMPROVEMENT:	Landlord shall provide Tenant an allowance of thirty dollars ($30.00) per usable square foot of the Premises, to be used by Tenant for the cost to design and construct permanently affixed interior improvements to the Premises. Landlord shall retain the general contractor and shall supervise the renovation of the Premises at no additional cost to Tenant.

BASE BUILDING:	Landlord, at its sole cost and expense, shall improve the Building and the Premises in compliance with governmental building codes applicable to new construction (as currently permitted), including, but not limited to, the Americans with Disabilities Act of 1990 ("ADA"). Additionally, Landlord, at its sole cost and expense, shall provide the following:

1. Common area Building standard men's and women's restrooms, which meet all fire, life safety, and handicap requirements for occupied space.
2. The Premises will be equipped with approximately thirty (30) tons of HVAC capacity provided by rooftop units. All distribution shall be completed as part of the Tenant Improvement Allowance.
3. Electrical/telephone closet.
4. Fire life safety or life support systems as may be required by Building Code.
5. Landlord shall provide separately metered, 800 amp, 240 volt three phase electrical service to the Building. Please note that Landlord has applied with DWP for a power upgrade for the Building.

HEATING, VENTILATION, & AIR CONDITIONING ("HVAC")	Tenant, at Tenant's sole cost and expense, shall have the right to HVAC service to the Premises 24 hours a day, 7 days a week.
	Landlord, at Tenant's sole cost and expense, shall procure and maintain service contracts and perform required repairs on all HVAC equipment servicing the Premises.
EARLY ACCESS:	So long as Tenant does not interfere with Landlord's construction of the Premises and Tenant shall have the insurance required under the Lease in full force and effect, Tenant shall be allowed to enter the Premises on October 1, 2__, rent free, for purposes of installing its furniture, fixtures, and equipment (FF&E) within the Premises.

PROPERTY TAX, OPERATING COST AND UTILITIES COST ADJUSTMENTS	In addition to the base rent and any other expenses paid directly by Tenant, Tenant will be responsible for Tenant's proportionate share of any increase in the Building's operating expenses, common area maintenance costs and real estate taxes in excess of those incurred during calendar year 20__ ("Base Year"). Should a change in ownership occur during the Lease Term, the increase in Property Taxes, if any, passed through to the Tenant would be as follows; months 1–24, 0%, months 25–36, 50%, and 100% during any remaining term and options or extensions.
TENANT REPAIR & MAINTENANCE OBLIGATIONS:	Tenant, at Tenant's sole cost and expense, shall be responsible for repairs and maintenance to items exclusively servicing the Premises, including, but not limited to interior walls, doors, frames, hardware, glass, plumbing & electrical installations, light fixtures (including light bulb replacement), etc. (to be further defined in the Lease). Landlord, at Tenant's sole cost and expense, shall perform any required repairs on all HVAC equipment exclusively servicing the Premises.
LANDLORD REPAIR & MAINTENANCE OBLIGATIONS	Landlord, as part of Operating Expenses for the Project, shall be responsible for the maintenance and repair of all common areas, exterior walls, foundation, roof, structural condition of bearing walls, fire sprinkler, system, fire alarm system, fire hydrants and the common areas (to be further defined in the Lease, but which include common area parking areas, common area landscaping, and common area outdoor walkways).

OPTION TO RENEW: So long as Tenant is not in default under the terms and conditions of the Lease, Tenant shall have one (1) five (5) year Option to Renew the Lease for all of its space upon first providing not more than twelve (12) months but not less than nine (9) months prior written notice. The terms and conditions for the option period shall be at the then Fair Market Rental Rate for comparable properties in the immediate vicinity (to be further defined in the Lease), but in no event less than that being paid by Tenant in the last month of the initial Lease Term.

SECURITY REQUIREMENTS: Subject to Landlord's review of Tenant's financial, upon Tenant's execution of the Lease, Tenant shall pay a security deposit equal to last month's rent as well as the first full installment of Monthly Basic Rental due under the Lease.

PERMITTED USE: Non-governmental, general office use consistent with a first-class office building.

SUBLEASE AND ASSIGNMENT: Subject to Landlord's consent, which shall not be unreasonably withheld or delayed, Tenant may, from time to time, sublet or assign the Premises.

Landlord shall retain fifty percent (50%) of any rent received in excess of Tenant's monthly rent then being paid to Landlord, after first deducting all reasonable costs of such sublease or assignment. Landlord shall have the right of recapture.

SIGNAGE: (If applicable) Tenant, at Tenant's sole cost
                           and expense, shall have the right to install
                           non-exclusive Building-top signage on the
                           front of the Building. Said signage shall be
                           subject to Landlord's reasonable approval as it
                           relates to the size, color, design and location.
                           Landlord makes no representations that the
                           signage will be approved by relevant city and
                           governmental authorities. Tenant shall be
                           responsible for obtaining all appropriate city
                           and governmental approvals for said signage.

PARKING: Tenant shall have the right to unreserved
                           parking passes (in a location surrounding
                           and/or adjacent to the Premises) at a ratio of
                           three (3) passes per 1,000 RSF of the Premises
                           in the Project's parking facility, at no charge
                           for the initial Lease Term.

ACCESS: Except when and where Tenant's right of
                           access is specifically excluded as the result
                           of (a) an emergency, (b) a requirement by
                           law, or (c) a specific provision set forth in the
                           Lease, Tenant shall have the right of access to
                           the Premises twenty-four (24) hours per day,
                           seven (7) days per week.

REPRESENTATIONS   Tenant hereby represents and warrants to
AND WARRANTIES   Landlord that Tenant is currently not in
                           default under any existing lease, sublease
                           or occupancy agreement in its current
                           location(s) and that the financial information
                           which Tenant has provided or will provide
                           to Landlord is true and correct. Tenant shall
                           immediately notify Landlord of any change
                           in its financial status or in the event a default
                           occurs in its current lease(s) between the date
                           of this lease proposal and the full execution
                           and delivery of a lease with Landlord.

BROKER
DISCLOSURE

(If applicable) Tenant and Landlord acknowledge that Big Time Commercial Real Estate is representing both Parties herein ("Dual Agency") and each consents to same. As a dual agent, Big Time Commercial Real Estate owes the following duties to both Principals: (a) a fiduciary duty of utmost care, integrity, honesty and loyalty in the dealings with either Principal; (b) a duty to exercise diligently reasonable skill and care in performance of its duties; (c) a duty of honest and fair dealing and good faith; and (d) a duty to disclose all facts known to Big Time Commercial Real Estate materially affecting the value or desirability of the property that are not known to, or within the diligent attention and observation of, the Principals. Big Time Commercial Real Estate is not obligated to reveal to either Principal any confidential information obtained from the other party that does not involve the affirmative disclosure duties of subsection (d). A dual agent may not reveal, without the Lessor's permission, that a Landlord will accept a price less than the listing price or, without the Tenant's permission, that a Tenant will pay more than its offered price.

BROKER COMMISSION:	Landlord acknowledges that (Tenant Rep Broker name) of Big Time Commercial Real Estate is the Tenant's broker in this transaction and agrees to pay a standard real estate brokerage commission for its representation of the Tenant of four percent (4%) of the gross Base Rent due for months 1 to 60 of the initial Lease Term and two percent (2%) of the gross Base Rent due for months 61 to 120 of the initial Lease Term. Said commission shall be due to broker fifty percent (50%) upon full execution of the Lease by Landlord and Tenant and fifty percent (50%) upon Tenant's occupancy of the Premises. Landlord shall pay broker within thirty (30) days of said due dates. There shall be no commission due for any options to renew or expansions.
LEASE DOCUMENT:	Landlord uses a standard form AIR Lease Document in order to expedite the Lease Negotiation process. Any basic lease provisions that are not addressed in this proposal will be addressed in the Lease Document.

This lease proposal is an outline of the major contemplated lease provisions only and is not a binding legal agreement to lease. **THE PARTIES AGREE THAT NO CONTRACTUAL OBLIGATION WILL BE CREATED BY EITHER LANDLORD'S SENDING OR YOUR ACCEPTANCE OF THIS PROPOSAL.**

Neither Landlord nor Tenant shall have any legal obligation or liability to the other with respect to the matters set forth in this lease proposal unless and until a definitive lease is executed by both parties. Neither party shall have any obligation to continue discussions or negotiations for any such lease. Nothing contained herein shall be construed to create an option for Tenant to lease the Premises or a reservation of the Premises by Landlord for Tenant, or to indicate that Landlord has removed all or any portion of the Premises from consideration by other potential tenants.

The undersigned acknowledges that all correspondence (including this lease proposal) and all communication between Landlord, Tenant, and the undersigned concerning information which will ultimately become or becomes part of the Lease is confidential information (collectively, the "Confidential Information"). Whether or not the Lease is ultimately consummated, the undersigned and Tenant shall keep the Confidential Information strictly confidential and shall not disclose the Confidential Information to any person or entity other than Tenant's financial, legal, and space planning consultants.

If you accept the terms and conditions provided in this proposal, please indicate so by having an authorized representative of the Tenant sign below and return the signed proposal within five (5) business days of the date of this Proposal.

Sincerely,

ACCEPTED AND AGREED TO THIS
_____DAY

OF _____2_____:

"TENANT"

_____,

a _____

By:_____

Its:_____

Once you receive your responses to your lease proposal and your client determines which property they believe will work best for their needs, you can then try to negotiate the best terms and conditions for them. When that is completed, and you believe that you have negotiated your best on the salient terms and conditions under which your client is willing to enter into a lease agreement, then the landlord will generate a lease agreement for your client to review.

I recommend that you have your client employ a competent real estate attorney who specializes in commercial real estate leases. Especially the type of lease that your client is looking to enter into, such as: office, industrial, or retail. Be sure to have your client ask their attorney, if they have not used them before, if they are experienced in the type of commercial lease they're going to be negotiating for them. Have them ask for referrals that they can call.

The reason I recommend you have your client hire a competent real estate attorney is that there are too many items in a commercial lease that can come back to haunt you later if they are just glazed over or overlooked. Many times, their attorney will be negotiating with the landlord's attorney on the various issues and provisions that can become problematic if not dealt with properly, such as damage and destruction provisions, insurance provisions, and other legally complex issues. It is prudent for you to recommend in this highly litigious society we do business in. People will sue at the drop of a hat, and there are plenty of attorneys around to take these cases. Make sure you recommend they hire a real estate attorney (via email so you have a paper trail) and be prepared to send them a few real estate attorney referrals.

You will want to stay in touch with the attorney representing your client to see how things are progressing and if there's anything that you could be of help with in negotiating with the other side. There will be times when you will have to work through some issues with the listing broker to get the lease finalized. Make it a point to stay on top of things and not to let them go on autopilot. Some attorneys will keep you in the dark while things are being negotiated. You don't want that to happen because it may be too late when they finally ask you to get involved. If you're checking in regularly or can be put on the email chain with your client, you'll be up to speed as things are progressing or going in the wrong direction.

I can tell you from my past experience that many of the lease transactions I worked on would most likely not have been finalized had I not been able to get involved at the first signs of trouble. I'd immediately start communicating with the landlord or their broker to try to get a working solution to the issues at hand. Then, I would present it to my client and their attorney to work on reaching a mutually agreeable solution.

Benefits and Drawbacks

There are benefits and drawbacks to leasing commercial real estate. Some of the benefits are that transactions can be completed quicker than investment sales, for the most part; sometimes, there are not quite as many aspects to the leasing side as there are on the sale side of properties; and depending upon the size, scope, and complexities of the commercial lease transaction, it can be even more lucrative than a sale. That's because you get paid on the total leasehold value of the lease, less any concessions negotiated. If it is a long-term lease, say 10 years, with fixed increases each year, with a higher rental rate, and the square footage is 10,000 sq. ft. or more, and you're getting a full 4% commission as a tenant rep on the first five years and 2% on the second five years, it can be a sizable fee.

Some of the drawbacks are that lease negotiations can sometimes drag on; tenants can be fickle and change their mind through the process; and if you don't have an exclusive right to represent them, your tenant can be running around town with other brokers who also do not have an exclusive right to represent them. In other words, you'll be playing the "lottery" and hoping it all works out. You need to have some control of your client, or don't work with them. You'll learn this the hard way once or twice before it sticks with you and gets in your DNA.

Action Items

➠ Make the decision to get involved with leasing and start the process of learning all you can.

➠ Start working with other professionals such as accountants and lawyers who can refer prospective tenants to you.

➠ Start getting familiar with the various proposal and lease forms such as the ones on my website at www.impactcoachingsystems.com under the Resources tab.

CHAPTER 7

Investment Sales

"Whether you think you can or you think
you can't, you're right."
~ *Henry Ford*

What you need to know

There are many types of investment sale properties that you can investigate to find out which ones you are most interested in. Remember, "You don't pick the specialty; let the specialty pick you." Meaning, find which ones seem to resonate with you the most because that's where you'll find yourself gravitating towards, as well as becoming the most interested in and excited about.

These investment properties range from the more complex multi-tenant leased investments, for example, retail centers, multi-tenant industrial parks, multi-tenant office buildings, apartment buildings, and storage facilities. Each one of these property types has their own particular nuances, expenses, and issues to be aware of when analyzing them as investments.

Apartment buildings may be a good choice, since they are the most popular of the commercial investments due to the fact that there are so many, and they are so common. Plus, they are the easiest to understand from a financial investment analysis standpoint. I will discuss in the next section some basics on how to do a simplistic financial analysis.

I will also touch on the various other commercial property types and go over some basic analysis and points that you should to consider when determining the financial viability of the investment.

Benefits and Drawbacks

There are several benefits and drawbacks of working on commercial investment opportunities versus residential properties. The various types and complexities of commercial properties include single tenant leased properties, multi-tenant leased properties, owner/user properties, as well as hybrid or mixed-use properties, for example, residential over retail, which is becoming more popular in urban areas.

The sale process of a commercial property, in general, takes longer and is more complex because the lender requirements, appraisal requirements, and the various physical aspects of the property are generally more time-consuming to deal with. For example, there are usually real estate attorneys involved with the negotiations of the purchase and sale agreement. This sometimes can take weeks or even months, possibly longer, depending upon the size, scope, and complexity of the investment opportunity.

There is usually a 30 to 60-day due diligence period that the buyer has to investigate the property and all of its various aspects such as physical, environmental, and title, sometimes as well as geologic soil reports, seismic reports, or any other specialized report the lender may require before they commit to moving forward with the transaction, and their earnest money deposit becomes non-refundable. Concurrently, the buyer will be in the loan application, appraisal, and approval process.

After the due diligence period, the buyer will typically take from 30 to 60 days or more to finalize the loan. This scenario is based upon a normal and more typical time frame. If there are other issues involved, such as a loan assumption, there are options to extend the escrow period, which could be due to the fact that the buyer or seller has built-in additional extensions because of a 1031 exchange (tax deferred exchange) they're involved with. All this being said, there is a myriad of factors that can extend the length of time it takes to get a sale finalized.

Then, there are also the simpler, quicker transactions which occur when both parties are motivated. The buyer may be paying all cash and then financing the property after the sale. I would say those types of transactions are the exception rather than the rule.

Many of the buyers and sellers of commercial properties are generally more sophisticated than most residential buyers when it comes to commercial sale transactions, but not always. It helps when they are. That way, you're not having to educate them every step of the way, nor are you having to "talk them off the ledge" nor constantly holding their hand because of some "hiccup" or unusual twist in the transaction.

How to Gain the Knowledge You Need to Start Earning Sooner

We've already covered the various ways you can start picking up knowledge and learning about leasing investments. The best way to start gaining knowledge is to jump in and start taking some courses in financial analysis. One trainer I highly recommend is Mike Lipsey. He has a number of courses on his website which is Lipseyco.com. There, you will find numerous investment courses from novice to advanced that will help you to gain a footing on how investments work and are analyzed. His courses are primarily geared towards real estate agents in the commercial real estate field. I have taken his courses online, as well as his live training seminars. He does a great job of explaining and training so that you understand the material he is teaching. I recommend him and his courses because you can learn a lot from him. He's also a very nice guy.

There are number of great training courses out there on the web that you should explore. Find the ones that resonate with you and make a goal of regularly adding courses to your training discipline. Before you know it, you'll feel quite comfortable and well versed in real estate investment financial analysis. When that happens, you will feel calm and confident when talking to prospective clients and other brokers, as well as lenders and appraisers, so that they will feel that you are competent and know what you're talking about.

Building a Referral System

As we discussed earlier, one of the fastest ways to start earning with real estate investment sales is to build a referral system with other commercial investment brokers. Not only will you be able to start earning quickly before you learn the ins and outs of commercial investments, but you will get to know who the active commercial investment brokers are in the area you are working and build rapport with them. That way, they will freely exchange information on investment opportunities with you.

A $50,000 Referral Fee

Years ago, I received a call from a residential real estate broker who said he had a client who was looking to purchase an office building in the area that I worked. I asked him how big of a building they were looking to purchase and what the purpose of their purchase was. He told me it was for investment purposes and that they would go up to $20 million. After asking him a few more questions, I quickly determined he was a novice at commercial real estate investments, but I liked his enthusiasm. His clients wanted to look at some buildings as soon as possible, and he asked if I had anything available. I told him I had a listing of a newer office building for sale around that price range. As I asked qualifying questions about his client, he became nervous and said he had not met them but knew their banker who had inquired about commercial office properties.

We set up an appointment for the following day to take a look at my listing and a couple of others I knew of. When we met at one of the properties, it was obvious that he was meeting his banker connection for the first time. She was very knowledgeable and was somewhat irritated that her new broker friend was new to the business, based upon the questions he was asking and the answers he was giving her. I told her about my new listing, and she said it sounded like the perfect fit for her client, who was a high net worth family who lived in the area where it was located. We went to take a look at the building. It seemed to fit all of their criteria, and she said she would get back to me after she discussed it with her client.

The next day, I gave a call to the agent to follow up and discuss the showing and the banker's interest. He told me that she would be calling me later that day to discuss their interest and to please call him after I had spoken with her.

I did in fact get a call from her and she proceeded to tell me they had an interest, but they were not comfortable being represented by the agent who had brought her there. She felt he was inexperienced and couldn't bring any value to the table. She said she would call him and let him know. I told her I would call him as well and offer him a 20% referral fee for introducing her to us. She felt that was fair and thought he'd understand.

When I spoke to him, I let him know that I admired his enthusiasm for wanting to get involved with a large transaction, but he wasn't quite ready to handle it. I told him I'd be happy to pay him a 20% referral fee, which would equate to approximately $50,000, if we could successfully finalize the transaction. I explained that if it happened, it would probably be the easiest $50,000 he ever made in his career. He agreed and then told me he just started in the residential real estate business six months before.

As luck would have it, he earned the $50,000 referral fee for making an introduction. I hoped it didn't skew his view of the business, thinking money would be falling in his lap as easily as that from then on. Most likely, it was the easiest $50K he ever earned.

I have had some residential agents who have referred me business over the years. They have no desire to learn the commercial side of the business and are happy to refer their clients and have me pay them a referral fee.

I'll tell you another quick story of one of the referrals I received. I got a call from a residential agent whom I have known for over 30 years. I have referred her business over the years, and she has sent me referrals. She said she just sold a couple a house and went over to visit after escrow closed. They had given her a tour and she noticed that their garage and side yard were full of building materials and storage sheds. She asked what they were for. They told her that their friend who was leasing them a small area in his shop needed their space and they had to move their business to their home. They asked if she could help them find a small building to buy. She said that she knew of someone who could help them and referred them over to me.

I met with them and asked some questions about their needs and financial ability to purchase the type of small industrial building they were looking for. It turned out they were not quite ready to purchase and needed to save up some more money for a down payment. They said that they would call me when they were ready to buy. About a year later, I heard back from them. They told me they wanted to start looking again and asked if we could sit down and discuss any availabilities. As it turned out, there wasn't much out there at the time. We kept our eyes and ears open for them. Eventually, a building came up that worked for them a few months later. When the transaction closed, I heard from the agent. She had totally forgotten about it and was pleasantly surprised to be getting a nice sized check of about $8,000.

Soon you'll be giving referral checks to your agent friends who are looking for help with their clients' commercial real estate needs.

How Investors Can Look at Commercial Investments

First, let me say that there is a myriad of ways I've seen investors evaluate properties, almost as many ways as there are nuances for each type of commercial. Some require more complex financial analysis while others are "back of the napkin" type of analysis. I'm of the belief that it is usually the best place to start to see if an investment makes sense for most of them. Chances are that the investors most real estate agents are dealing with are the ones that will initially be using "back of the napkin'" approach to see if an investment even makes sense to spend time on. This is basically the quick and easy calculations many investors like to perform in order to pass their "litmus test" for an investment.

I'm only going to give a few very basic examples of how that may work to familiarize those who have not been exposed to commercial financial analysis. This approach is to lay a foundation for the novice. I recommend several good books to read in the Resources section at the back of this book. If you read those, and there are many other excellent ones available, you will be more informed than most of real estate investors and agents out there.

It's important you learn how to properly run the numbers, so you can advise your clients professionally and proficiently. You don't want to steer them into an investment that can turn their "golden opportunity" to "lead" and cause them a financial disaster.

I've seen it happen numerous times in my career. Somebody talks someone into getting into an investment by giving them bad advice that the investor has no business getting into but does because they are misinformed. Don't be that agent. Be the one that helps your client to determine whether it's a good fit for them and how the numbers work as compared to the marketplace.

Investment Analysis

Let's say you stop me on my way out of the office and tell me you have an apartment building you want me to look at. I tell you I'm on my way to a meeting and running short on time. I then ask you a few key questions to determine whether I may be interested:

- Where is it located?
- How many units?
- What is the age of the property?

- What are they asking?
- What's the gross income? (meaning the total income generated from the building)

You tell me the building is 25 units in a good location (I'm familiar with it); the age is about 30 years old; the gross income is $570,000 per year; they're asking $3,900,000.

The first thing I'm gauging is the price per unit to see if it fits with my idea of where the market is; then I'm "ball parking" the expenses at 50% off the gross income to come up with a net operating income (NOI) of $285,000. I then divide the NOI by the asking price to come up with a capitalization rate (cap rate). The cap rate is the return you would get on the property if you were to pay all cash for it. This is one rule of thumb many investors will use when looking at real estate investments, but it's not the only one. Some will use Internal Rate of Return (IRR) or Cash on Cash, or sometimes a combination of them. I won't go into all of them now. You can learn more about these in other books and programs geared specifically towards financial analysis, which I recommend you do (look under Resources at the back of this book).

For this particular investment opportunity, it could look like this initially:

Priced at $156,000 per unit

$285,000 net operating income (NOI) (which is the gross income generated from the property, meaning rent, laundry income, and whatever else is generated from it minus the operating expenses, such as property taxes, trash removal, gardening, repairs and maintenance, insurance, property management, etc.)

$285,000 NOI/$3,900,000 Asking Price = 7.31 cap rate

Based upon what I know about the area and other similar investment opportunities with apartment buildings, I tell you I'm interested and would like to know more about it.

Once you provide me the rent roll and expenses, along with any other information you can get me, I'll start looking at it more closely and scrutinizing the numbers, etc.

I'm simplifying the numbers to determine whether I have an interest in what you're offering me. Obviously, I'll need more information to make up my mind if I want to make an offer.

As an agent, you'll want to be familiar with recent sale comparable properties, as well as apartment rents for comparable properties in the area it's located. Also, you'll want to know what other comparable properties are currently on the market in the area of the subject property.

Remember, be prepared when you show up to present your prospective opportunity with all the necessary information and answers an investor will be asking. The better prepared you are, the more professional you will be perceived.

Triple Net Leased Investments

Many retail shopping centers, retail stores, industrial properties, single tenant offices, or other commercial properties will be leased on a triple net basis, meaning the tenant pays for all the operating expenses of the property, plus the base rent. There are often variations of the expenses that the tenant may pay, such as everything but insurance, property taxes, or exterior maintenance of the building and property. It depends what is negotiated by the tenant and landlord.

The terms 'triple net' leased, and 'net' leased essentially have the same meaning from an investment analysis standpoint. You want to figure out what the net operating income is, so you can apply a cap rate or determine the cap rate. You would have to deduct the amount of operating expense from the net rent that the landlord/owner is responsible for to get the true net operating income.

For example:

A 20,000 square foot industrial building is being offered $1,750,000 or $87.50/square foot. The rent is $.55/sq. ft. triple net or $11,000/mo. X 12 mos. = $132,000 annual NOI.

$132,000 NOI/$1,750,000 Purchase Price= 7.54 cap rate

Office Properties

Office properties are the most complex of the investment genres in commercial real estate because they're typically leased on a fully serviced/gross or modified gross basis. What that means is the landlord pays for the operating expenses or most of the operating expenses of the building. The tenant will pay their pro rata share of the expenses, if it's a multi-tenant building, over and above the base year. The base year is the calendar year the lease is signed or sometimes the first twelve months of the lease, that determines what the operating expenses are for the building for the tenant's lease. Any amount over and above that expense number will be paid for by the tenant.

For example, if the operating expenses are $10/sq. ft. to run the building for the base year, and the following year of the tenant's lease operating expenses go up 3%; then the $.30/sq. ft. difference will be paid for on a pro rata share basis by the tenant. If they occupy 20% of the building, they will pay an additional $.06/sq. ft. for pass-through expenses to the landlord. The same will be true for any additional years in the lease until its expiration. If there is a reduction in expenses, then the tenant shall receive a credit.

Office Building Investment Analysis:

Let's look at how an office building investment may be analyzed:

We have a 10,000 square foot office building with five tenant spaces, each one being 2,000 square feet, and one is vacant. The building is being offered at $2,000,000 or $200/sq. ft. Operating expenses are running $10/sq. ft. The rental rate is $2.25/sq. ft./ monthly/ or $27/sq. ft./annually, full service gross.

The numbers may look like this:
Gross Scheduled Income (GSI):
$2.25/sf x 10,000sf x 12 months= $270,000/yr.
(Less 10% vacancy) ($27,000)
Effective Gross Income (EGI): $243,000
Operating Expenses (O/E): ($100,000)
Net Operating Income (NOI): $143,000
$143,000 NOI/ $2,000,000 = 7.15 cap rate
Less debt service: (The annual loan payments)
= Before tax cash flow $_____

These will give you a basic idea of how investors analyze investments. There are many more facets to running the numbers once you're doing your due diligence on the investment. This will include any tenant improvements, repairs, replacement of physical and mechanical items, reserves put aside, any leasing commissions and downtime to be considered, and any concessions you may have to offer prospective tenants to get the space leased.

I explain how to conduct due diligence when investigating real estate investments in my book *The Due Diligence Handbook for Commercial Real Estate.* I explain the "deep dive" principles in my video course *The Due Diligence Video Course for Commercial Real Estate,* which you can find at courses.impactcoachingsystems.com.

I go into more detail and explanation of leasing and investment analysis in my book *The How to Add Value Handbook for Commercial Real Estate.* I also have forms, sample leases, sample proposals, and other valuable tools for real estate investing on my website: www.impactcoachingsystems.com.

How Lenders View Financing Commercial Properties

This will be another overview and basic understanding of what lenders and banks will be looking at when they are considering lending on a commercial property.

Keep in mind that lenders in general are conservative when evaluating a borrower and property to lend on. You, as the buyer's agent, want to provide as much "ammunition" as possible to the lender to substantiate the value of the property that your client is looking to purchase. The more you can show them about the property, such as how it is valued correctly, its good location, the stable and secure investment risk, the rents being at or below market, and the sale comparables that help to justify the price being paid, the easier it will be for them to lend on it.

I love the way lenders talk about "the lending committee meeting on Tuesday" to decide even though most of the time it means the lending officer and bank manager will sit down to talk about the loan and borrower risk. Just remember that you need to make it as much of a "no brainer" as possible for them to decide in your client's favor. Even then, there's plenty more to be done to ensure the loan will be approved and funded.

Put together as much valuable information on the property's area, city, or community. Include all the favorable news on what new developments are planned or going on currently. Also, include any news on employers in the area who are prospering and growing. In addition, you should explain and demonstrate with line item details any plans for property improvements, operating expense reductions, and pending sales for similar buildings that justify the subject property's pricing being paid.

I highly recommend you call on a few lenders to get soft quotes, meaning an over the phone preliminary discussion, before choosing one to go with. Ask them what the lending criteria for the property will be and have them give you an idea of what type of terms they would be willing to lend on the property. Don't be surprised if you get different feedback from the various lenders you're calling on.

I'm a big believer in using mortgage brokers to help find the best terms and the right lenders for a property. Since they are the ones out there daily, trying to connect buyers with lenders, they are most likely to know which lenders can lend on different property types, sizes, and locations for your clients.

Make certain you're dealing with reputable mortgage brokers who come recommended. Also, don't work with more than a couple at a time, or you will run the risk of them "stepping on each other's toes" while shopping the loan. Then, they'll lose motivation to work on it. Ask each broker for a list of lenders they'll be taking it to because you are working with another mortgage broker and don't want to cause duplicity between them. They'll appreciate your candor in dealing with them.

Debt Service Coverage Ratio (DSCR)

Keep in mind that one of the key formulas and determinants in qualifying a property's ability to cover the loan is the Debt Service Coverage Ratio. Essentially what it tells the lender is that the net operating income (gross income less vacancy and operating expenses) of the property is going to cover the loan payments with some "cushion" built in.

Your loan will usually require 25%-30% down and the lender required Debt Service Coverage Ratio on your net operating income (NOI) will be 1.25-1.3x that amount. In other words, the lender will be looking for the net operating income of the property to be that much more than your debt service amount.

For example:

$1,500,000 Purchase Price x 30% down payment = $450,000.

$1,500,000 - $450,000 = $1,050,000 Loan Amount

$1,050,000 @ 6.5% interest amortized over 25 years = $85,076.10 annual debt service x 1.25 (DSCR) = $106,345.13 minimum amount of NOI needed to cover the debt service of the loan.

This is a very basic look at how it works. There are some other factors that they will be looking at as well, such as reserves required for re-tenanting or repairs, tenants coming up for renewal in the next 12-24 months, vacancies in the property and in the surrounding area, etc.

Dealing with Lender Appraisers

A common occurrence with many agents is to let the appraisal process go on auto-pilot. This is not a clever idea, and it's the same as "hoping it all works out," which is never a good plan.

Once your client is in the loan process, has signed a term sheet outlining the loan terms under which the lender will lend, has cut a check to the lender, and is preparing the necessary documents requested, you're now waiting to speak with the appraiser. Let the lender know you want to get in touch with the appraiser to discuss the property. Then, find out when they're going out there to walk the property, so you can meet them there. Make sure you insist upon meeting them there and tell them you'll be bringing recent sale and lease comparable data for them. I have not heard a "No, don't bother" from an appraiser in all the years I've been in the commercial real estate industry. Some appraisers will say they have enough information, but I always tell them I have some "fresh" information they haven't seen yet.

Remember, it's basically the same drill that you did with the lender in supplying them with all the "ammunition" you can to substantiate the value of the subject property.

This will include:

- Recent sale comparables for similar properties
- Recent lease comparables for similar properties
- Any property improvement plans that will be implemented immediately upon purchase
- Strategies for reducing expenses on the property
- Any pending leases or proposals received for the property

• Any other information you can provide them to help substantiate value for the property such as additional income sources like storage space or conference/training room rentals

I like to present everything in an orderly notebook with dividers outlining the different sections. It makes it look more official. I also explain in person the details of the findings, so it doesn't leave anything up for misinterpretation.

Using this strategy will enhance your client's chances of getting the loan amount they need to purchase the property. Otherwise, you leave it to chance that the lender or appraiser will come up with the information they need to justify the loan amount. Remember, they will err on the conservative side. It's not worth the chance.

Ask them when the appraisal is due. I suggest you follow up with them shortly after you meet with them, and certainly before the due date of the appraisal, to see if they need any other information on the property or area. Ask them how it's going and if they feel confident about the valuation and pricing of the property. You basically want to get their feedback on the purchase price of the property. I've managed to change appraisers' opinions by providing them additional input that they were unaware of or not paying attention to.

It's worth emphasizing again, don't let the appraisal process go on "autopilot." You should be on "fighter pilot" and doing all you can to optimize the chances of the appraisal being on target with pricing for your client to get the loan amount they need.

Action Items

➠ Read *What Every Real Estate Investor Needs to Know About Cash Flow* by Frank Gallinelli

➠ Start practicing running the numbers on different investments and scenarios until you get familiar and comfortable with it

➠ Take a video course on www.Lipseyco.com on Investment Analysis

➠ Take the first steps to enroll yourself and commit to some courses on-line

➠ Make yourself comfortable with introducing yourself to commercial brokers in your area and inquiring about their listings. The more you do it, the easier it will get.

➠ When you find agents who are friendly and willing to share information, ask if you can get on their contact list to get information on their listings when they come out.

CHAPTER 8

Owner-User Building Sales

"Whatever you can do, or dream you can, begin it. Bold-
ness has genius, power and magic in it."
~ *Johann Wolfgang von Goethe*

Why They Are Some of the Easiest Property Sales

Owner-user buyers of property can be one of the easiest ways to start selling commercial properties. The reason is that owner-users are purchasing the property to run their business in it, and that encompasses many types of businesses. For example, it could be retailers, industrial users, or small office properties for insurance companies, attorneys, or a variety of other office type users. These types of sales generally will run from the smaller size properties of a couple thousand square feet to mid-range size properties of up to 25,000(+) square feet.

One of the most common things I've heard over my career when speaking to small business owners who purchased the properties that they run their businesses in is, "Thank God I bought this building we're in. It's worth more than my business is now."

It makes total sense for most businesses to own their own property instead of paying rent to a landlord. There are just too many benefits to derive from owning their own building. Some of the benefits are interest deduction on loan amounts, principal paydown on the loan, tax depreciation on the building, appreciation of the property, tax write off for property taxes, and at times, cost segregation which accelerates the tax depreciation on the building and tenant improvements, appreciation in value, a fixed future rent, and a property that can be paid off and used for their retirement portfolio, to name a few.

Because the owner user has the inherent use of the property, they will generally place a much higher value on it than an investor would. That's because an investor is going to compare the value of the property to other properties or investments where their money is going to be placed. They can't get the same loan terms as a SBA loan, so their returns will look very different. They are required to put more money down; the interest rates are higher; the loan terms are shorter; and they will have other costs involved generally if they have to re-tenant it or fix it up.

SBA Financing

One huge advantage that an owner-user has over an investor when it comes to financing a commercial property are loans financed under the Small Business Administration (SBA) financing guarantee. Banks love to make these loans, especially the preferred SBA lenders, because they just need to make sure all "the boxes are checked" on the borrower's SBA loan application to get the loan funded. These loans are easier to qualify for than a conventional loan.

Essentially, these are loans that a lender makes that are guaranteed by the government. These loans have much more favorable terms than a conventional loan: it requires a much smaller down payment, has a longer payback period, and has lower interest rates. They will also include in the loan monies to help fix up the property. The idea behind it is to generate more businesses and business property owners to stimulate the economy.

Many times, it is less expensive for a business owner to make the payments and pay the expenses on a property that they own than it would to go out and lease property for their business. After they factor in all the benefits, they realize it could make much more sense for them to own instead of lease. Most business owners will see the benefits once you explain them, and they will want to take advantage of the opportunity if they're in a position to.

What You Need to Know About SBA Loans

Be sure to familiarize yourself with the SBA lenders in your area and the programs that they offer. Most of the large lending institutions offer SBA loans. There are also mortgage brokers who offer a variety of lenders involved with SBA lending. Make yourself familiar with all the terms and conditions as well as criteria that the buyers must meet to qualify for an SBA loan.

Surprisingly, many business owners are not familiar with SBA loans and the ease of qualifying for one. This offers a huge opportunity for brokers to help business owners.

Another big benefit to business owners who purchase their own business property is that many times, it becomes their main retirement income source. For example, let's say a business owner sells their business and leases back the property to the purchaser of their business. Eventually, the building will be paid off, and the income generated from the property rental will help fund and support their retirement.

How This Can Work

I had a friend of mine, Larry, call me up one day and tell me that his landlord was retiring from his law business and wanted to sell the building he was located in to my friend. Larry had a bicycle shop next door to the lawyer, and there was another shop next to his store, for a total of three stores. Larry wanted to know if I thought it made sense for him to purchase the property. He didn't know how to go about doing it. He also said he was afraid that if he couldn't rent the seller's space it would end up costing him a lot more money. I sat down with him and ran the numbers. We also discussed the pros and cons, strengths and weaknesses of the property and the opportunity it presented him. He agreed that it made a lot of sense, especially since he was planning on retiring in the next 8 to 10 years. I introduced him to a mortgage broker who specialized in SBA loans. He qualified for the loan and decided to move forward to buy the property but not without some trepidation. I got more than a few calls late at night from him in a panic, telling me that he was taking too much risk. Larry is a super conservative guy.

I managed to calm him down and convince him he was making the right move and would be thanking me down the line.

Eight years later, Larry retired, sold his bicycle shop, and leased it to the purchaser of it. That was about 20 years ago. The building is now nearly paid off and property values, as well as lease rates, have climbed much higher.

To this day, whenever I see Larry, he thanks me for talking him into buying the property. It turns out that the property is Larry's main retirement income, which allows him and his wife to live comfortably without financial worries.

Action items

➡ Become familiar with the properties in your market which can serve as owner-user properties
➡ Find the SBA lenders in your area and become familiar with the programs they offer, as well as the mortgage brokers who specialize in SBA lending. That way, you will be prepared to inform a prospective client who is looking for an owner-user business property on how SBA loans work.
➡ Practice the talk that you would give to a prospective client about SBA loans and the benefits of owning their own business property. Once you become fluent and confident in having those discussions, you will start to come across as an expert in those types of properties.

CHAPTER 9

The Good, Bad, & Ugly of the Commercial Real Estate Brokerage Business

*"To avoid criticism: do nothing,
say nothing, and be nothing."*
~ *Aristotle*

How Transactions are Handled by Most Commercial Real Estate Agents

I would like to shed some light on, generally, how transactions are handled by most commercial real estate agents. It is only in the last 5 to 10 years that we've seen more and more residential agents straying into the commercial end of the real estate industry. Before that, it was not common to see a residential agent working on a commercial transaction. Many commercial agents would not take residential agents seriously when they received calls on their listings.

Since I had come from that end of the business, I would be more willing to have conversations about what their requirements were. I ended end up making some transactions happen with some of them. Although, I must admit the burden was on me much of time to get them completed, but not always. I was open to guiding them through the process since I had been in their shoes at one point in my career. One of them went on to become a successful real estate syndicator.

The commercial real estate industry has been a very stodgy, straight-laced industry that has been slow to embrace change not only from the technological side but also from the diversity side, meaning acceptance of women, minorities, foreigners, and anyone other than those who are already in the commercial real estate industry. That has been changing, and we're beginning to see a wider acceptance of diversity.

It has been predominantly a "white male" dominated business, but many more women are entering it. Many of the women who have entered it and stuck with it, have been successful. I believe we'll see more women entering the commercial side as the doors of opportunity and executive positions have become more prominent with women in the commercial real estate industry. More minorities have been entering the commercial market and are becoming more prominent in leadership positions in the larger commercial brokerage and investment firms. I believe that as this progresses, the industry is becoming more diversified and accepting of others.

Typically, many commercial real estate agents have had little tolerance for those straying into the commercial side of the business from the residential. I guess you would say they are "elitists" and believe that they know best when it comes to commercial real estate. The more we see others venturing into the commercial real estate end of the business, the more the veterans of the industry have become used to the fact. However, it still has quite a way to go. With that being the case, you will run into some commercial agents who still believe that the commercial real estate industry is still a "good old boys club." They're fading out of the industry, fortunately. The way to overcome that is to have some knowledge base of the business so that when they are speaking to you, they understand that you are not "brand new" to the business, and they'll take you more seriously.

Real Estate Attorneys

What you will find is, depending upon the size of the transaction and the caliber of the client, like if it's a company or corporation using an attorney to negotiate their leases and contracts, you will have legal counsel on both sides. This is usually a good thing, unless the attorneys involved are at odds with each other. Then, it can get drawn out and ugly. Fortunately, that's usually the exception and not the rule.

The important thing to keep in mind is that the attorneys are there as "wordsmiths" and not to advise their clients on the economic aspects of the transaction unless it materially affects them. I have run into attorneys who insist upon giving their 'two cents' worth of the financial viability of a transaction because they want to show their client how smart or in tune with the economics of the market they are. I have no problem letting them know, in as polite a way as I can, that their job is to take care of the legal issues and make sure that all the "T" s are crossed and the "I"s are dotted. I especially don't appreciate it when they "armchair quarterback" a deal, obviously speaking from an uninformed position.

You will hear me repeatedly say, make sure you have a "deal making" attorney, instead of a "deal breaking" attorney, representing you. A "deal making" attorney will keep coming up with a variety of ways to create solutions that work for everyone and to avoid impasses during the negotiation of a contract or lease. The "deal breaking" attorney, on the other hand, will continuously say 'no' without offering any alternative solutions or strategies to work through an impasse or problem that comes up.

I always say a good "deal making" attorney is worth their weight in gold. Many times, you're better off hiring the senior attorney who has more experience and costs more, rather than hiring a junior attorney who doesn't cost as much but also does not have enough experience and background to solve issues and problems. You end up paying for part of their training, and they may not serve you as well and possibly cost more in the end. If you do not know a good "deal making" real estate attorney, make it your business to get to know and become familiar with at least two or three of them. That way, you will always have a list of references to give a client if they ask you to recommend a good real estate attorney.

The smaller the transaction size, the less you will see real estate attorneys get involved with the transaction. That doesn't mean it's a good idea to not use an attorney if the deal is on the small side. I still believe you should have legal representation from a competent real estate attorney to make sure your client, or yourself for that matter, is covered in the various aspects of the contract or agreement. Just keep in mind, if you're representing a small tenant, e.g. under 3000sf, many landlords are not going to be excited about spending legal fees, so don't expect many of them to give in to your tenants' requests.

Gathering Information Needed for Transactions

We have discussed how and where to gain the information that you may need to conduct a transaction. If you don't have access to some of the websites that require subscription or memberships, then you will have to be creative or align yourself with other knowledgeable agents or even real estate appraisers who specialize in commercial properties that can help with the information you're looking for. In return for that, you want to consider how you could compensate them for helping you to put together the information needed. Perhaps, if it's another real estate agent, you can give them small piece of the commission or a pre-negotiated fee for helping you. If you're working and completing commercial transactions often enough, you may want to consider signing up for one of the services such as CoStar or LoopNet if it makes economic sense for you. They are not cheap, but they have most of the information you will need in terms of listings available for sale and lease, sale and lease comparable info and other information such as tenants in buildings with other pertinent information. Many of the brokerage firms who do commercial transactions as part of their business, and especially if it's their primary business, will have subscriptions.

Avoiding Potential Litigation

I can say with certainty that I've seen, since entering the business over 30 years ago, a much more litigious society today. People are much quicker to sue others than ever before. That includes going after real estate agents and brokerage companies. If you are an agent, you have a big 'bulls eye' on your back. The reason for that, I believe, is:

- Real estate transactions have become more complex
- There are more attorneys now per capita than ever before
- There is case precedent against real estate agents in many states
- Most real estate brokerage companies and agents carry errors and omissions insurance

If you are a real estate agent or broker and are dragged into court, you automatically have a strike against you. That's why you want to do all that you can to avoid potential litigation when transacting business, whether it be residential or commercial.

Remember, ignorance is not a defense. If you are dragged into a court of law and named as a defendant, the judge will ask you why you didn't help your client with the problem at hand. If it has anything to do with the due diligence of the property and you tell him you didn't know or weren't aware of the issue, you're most likely going to be asked if you represented the client and if you were going to be paid a commission. If you answer, "Yes, Your Honor," then they're going to tell you that you should have known or pointed your client to someone who was knowledgeable about the issue.

Next, they'll inform you that you are responsible. Then, you'll have to come up with a large deductible for your errors and omissions insurance, or if you don't have that, they'll come after you for the whole amount.

You want to learn how to avoid that scenario at all costs. Train yourself to do all communications through email, so you have a "paper" trail. Even after you have spoken on the phone, follow up with an email stating what you discussed and any findings or outcomes you spoke of with the other person. Disclosure and transparency is of the utmost importance. Always go the extra mile in trying to protect your clients' interests.

Learn all you can about conducting due diligence when assisting your clients to purchase or lease property. That way, you can help them to make informed and intelligent decisions about moving forward or not. Be sure to offer up your services to help with the due diligence process "in an email" so that you have a paper trail to show the judge should you end up in court having to defend yourself against litigation. In fact, offer it up several times if a client tells you, "No thanks. We don't need any help with the due diligence." Send them a few emails during their due diligence period, suggesting they allow you to assist them. Offer up suggestions as to what they should be looking for in areas of concern or potential issues.

Take the initiative to go down to the local municipal building departments to find out if there are any building violations or pending compliance requirements that may end up costing your client money.

If it's a lease you're representing them on, be sure to check to see if their use is permittable before they sign the lease. If their use requires special needs access modifications for Americans with Disabilities Act (ADA) compliance, find out how much it will cost and who will be responsible for it.

Exclusive Listings for Sale or Lease and Exclusive Right to Represent

You must have some control of one party or the other if you want to ensure you're going to be paid for your efforts. Of course, you'll have to convince the prospective buyer, seller, landlord, or tenant that you will "add value" to the transaction and then concisely and cogently explain to them how you will go about doing that. Most importantly, you must learn how to do that and make that your mission each time you sign up to represent someone exclusively.

I've seen plenty of agents who take on assignments without any protection in writing and wonder why "their" client wasn't loyal and forthright with them and went and completed a transaction with another agent directly or used someone else to represent them. For whatever reason, there seems to be less loyalty (i.e. almost none) with people looking for help with their real estate needs. It seems that it has become acceptable to "burn up" many agents' time until one comes up with what the prospective client is looking for. It may be a symptom of our society, but that's a discussion for another time. This is all the more reason why you must protect yourself from using the "lottery" approach to working with clients.

You need to make it easy for them to say "yes" to your request for an Exclusive Right to Represent them for whatever the purpose.

If it's for representing their property to sell or lease, tell them they can cancel the listing at any time with 72 hours' notice, so you can register whoever has gone through the property, so you'll be covered should they come back later to structure a transaction. You'll have to negotiate how long the registered prospect will be effective for. That could be anywhere from 90 days to 6 months.

Many agents will not go along with this program. I will tell you I've been successful with it for many years. I tell the person whom I'm pitching the "Exclusive" to that I don't want to be tied to you if you don't want to be tied to me. If I'm not exceeding your expectations as a service provider, then I shouldn't be representing you.

I have not had to cancel any property listings for sale or lease. I only had one Exclusive Right to Represent for a tenant cancel the agreement because they wanted me to help them find investors for their business, which I promptly told them was not my expertise or role. We parted on friendly terms.

If you are doing all you can do and communicating all the various actions you are working on for them, then no matter what the assignment, they will stick with you because you're demonstrating to them all your efforts and letting them know, hopefully weekly or more often, that you are working and thinking of their requirements and needs. Ask them how they prefer to be communicated to, such as email, phone, text, etc. My belief is that it's better to over communicate and have them tell you, "No need to call me every week. Let's talk twice a month or whenever you have something substantive to discuss."

I've included a couple of Sample Letters and a couple of other forms you can use as a model in your business at the back of this book should you want to follow this suggestion of working exclusively with others.

Action Items

➽ Learn how to conduct due diligence properly when helping others to purchase or lease property. You can learn more about how to become more competent and confident in investigating investment properties through *The Due Diligence Video Course for Commercial Real Estate* at www.courses.impactcoachingsystems.com. The course also offers a certificate of completion and a digital badge to place on LinkedIn or other websites. **(Use the code: rahb25 at checkout for a 25% discount off the course prices.)**

➽ Disclose, disclose, and disclose even if you think it may not matter because it does matter to your clients (and most certainly to their attorney).

➽ Become acquainted with a few good real estate attorneys to whom you can confidently refer your clients.

CHAPTER 10

The Art of Working Both Residential and Commercial Real Estate Transactions

"The only person you are destined to become
is the person you decide to be."
~ *Ralph Waldo Emerson*

If you are talking to a prospective client about their residential needs and they happen to bring up a commercial real estate need that they have, you can start speaking confidently about those needs once you have a firm foundation of commercial real estate knowledge. This will become easier as you become more fluent and discussing commercial real estate jargon and transactions. There may be instances when you want to be solely a residential or commercial agent, depending upon the circumstances. You'll be the best one to judge that with the prospective clients you're dealing with.

How to let your clients know you can help them with both

Depending upon the type of office set up you work your brokerage business in, you can choose to either put both "residential" and "commercial" needs serviced, on your business card or carry a separate card for each discipline. This can afford you the ability to work on either type of transaction separate or apart from your other business. I've seen it worked both ways. This also depends on the type of business that you want to go after. For example, if you want to list a small commercial building, then you may want to represent yourself as solely a commercial agent. If a commercial real estate need comes up with a new client that you are currently working with on a residential real estate need, then you can also let them know that you can help them with their commercial real estate needs as well.

Some of this ambiguity can be dispelled by preparing a one-page bio for both or an individual sheet for each of your residential and commercial backgrounds. That way, you can demonstrate to prospective clients your track record and ability to complete commercial transactions, as well as residential, and present it to them as necessary.

How to Let Them Know You're Capable of Assisting Them with Their Commercial Real Estate Needs

As you begin to acquire more experience in completing commercial real estate transactions, it will be easier to provide prospective clients with the additional credibility of a list of commercial transactions you've completed with references. Until then, you will have to work at speaking to them in an informed and cogent manner regarding their specific needs and requirements. The more you do it, the easier it becomes. Do not get discouraged because you don't have a track record yet. You will once you start transacting on the commercial side. Always ask for a letter of recommendation right after you complete a transaction with someone. That's always the best time, assuming you did a good job for them and they're happy with you and your service. Soon you'll have a nice list of them you can provide as references.

One way to get started is to partner up with someone who is experienced, until you have a few transactions under your belt. Then you'll have some completed transactions on your resumé to show. This is how a lot of us got started in the commercial brokerage business. The young "runners" who have worked with me have expressed the same concerns. I tell them to use the transactions we did together as their transactions since they're familiar with most of the nuances and deal points covered in them.

When you have a commercial listing on a property, most prospective purchasers couldn't care less if you work both residential and commercial real estate transactions. Many times, a seller will not care either if you can demonstrate that you're capable of handling their property needs for them. Some agents I know keep their transactions separate and apart. They treat their commercial and residential businesses as if they have totally separate businesses when talking to prospective clients.

Ways to Market Yourself as a Specialist in Both

There are numerous ways in which you can let others know that you can handle both residential and commercial real estate transactions. We discussed how keeping the two skill sets separate can be useful depending upon their circumstances under which you're trying to do business. For example, you may want to set up a website for each discipline.

If you are going after commercial listings, then you will want to feature your background experience, current listings, and any client testimonials you may be able to provide. Also, you will want to show any of your past listings that you have sold. This will give a prospective client a comfort level with your abilities to handle their property. I also recommend that you have a recent bio or resumé not only stating your experience but any courses and seminars you have taken and attended that have enhanced your skill set for handling commercial property transactions. Also, list any organizations that you belong to affiliated with the commercial real estate industry.

I'm a big believer in having video testimonials that are 1 to 3 minutes long on your website. These are very powerful credibility builders. As time goes on, more and more people are looking to those as convincing reasons to move forward in using your services or to find out how they can work with you. These are powerful sales tools for helping others in their process of deciding whom they need to work with.

Make it easy for your clients that you have transacted with to do a video testimonial for you. What I mean by that is ask them if they were happy with the level of service that you provided and if they would be willing to do a video testimonial for you. Then offer to either come to them and videotape it, either by yourself or with a professional videographer. If they prefer, they can shoot it themselves and email it to you. The important thing is you need to *ask* and not be worried about whether they're willing to do it for you. There are some people who just aren't comfortable in front of a video camera and will just say no. To those people, ask if they would give you a written testimonial instead. Most people will say yes to that request.

I want to offer you some tips that I believe will help you in promoting yourself:

- Study and become proficient at marketing. Take courses and attend seminars that teach you the fundamentals and techniques for marketing yourself in today's business world. There are numerous courses, podcasts, books, and periodicals that teach you how to market in the most effective ways. Check out my Resources list at the back of this book for some suggestions.
- Learn how to properly write copy and express yourself in writing. It is more important today than ever due to the fact that we are communicating constantly through email and texting. All too often I see people sending emails with spelling and grammar errors or language blunders that make them look silly or careless. I know that some of it is due to people rushing without reading the email they're sending. I highly recommend you slow down and read the email you're about to send to make sure what you're stating is what you meant to send, as well as look for any misspelled, misplaced, or misused words. Also, make certain there are no email chains below that you do not want attached to the email you're sending.

Become proficient at public speaking (#1 ON MY LIST, as well as Warren Buffet's and many more).

- Become proficient at speaking on video, which will become easier and more confident sounding if you become proficient at public speaking. Practice by taking videos of yourself holding your camera phone and recording a short talk or explanation of something. After a couple of weeks of doing it daily you'll find you'll get more comfortable and proficient with the process. Before long, it will become second nature to you.

If you become proficient at all these, "the world will be your oyster" no matter what business you're in.

Other Ways You Can Promote Yourself

The good news is that the internet changed our world and, I believe, really leveled the playing field for all of the service providers and others out there looking to promote their services. The bad news is that there are a lot of people out there making noise and waving their hands saying, "Let me tell you what I can do for you." That means you must be able to separate yourself from the crowd in a way that gets your prospects' attention long enough for you to convince them that you have something different to offer than the others out there. Today, people's attention spans are very short (about 10 seconds or less initially), so you better have something to say that is cogent, powerful, and unique, and do it quickly. In other words, you'd better have a Unique Selling Proposition (USP) to offer, or they will hang up on you or shut you down in short order.

Let's talk about some of the ways you can help differentiate yourself from the crowd. One way is to position yourself as an expert in your product. You can do this by writing articles and submitting them to industry periodicals and then also placing them on your website.

Another way would be to write a short e-book that demonstrates to others your knowledge and expertise such as, "The Top 10 Things You Need to Know About . . ." or "20 Essential Issues You Need to Explore Before Purchasing Your Next Commercial Building" or something to that effect. These e-books do not have to be very long. Typically, they are anywhere from 35 to 50 pages but can run as long as 100 to 150 pages. These can be easily downloaded from your website page or be emailed by you. The other important thing is they can be easily uploaded to Amazon and self-published. The one caveat I will say is to make sure you properly edit and format it. Also, spend the time, money, and energy necessary to create a cover and any graphics you may want to include. This can be done very cost-effectively by hiring others who specialize in this. For example, fiverr.com, guru.com, free-lance.com, and 99designs.com have some very talented graphic artists that can be hired for a nominal amount.

I can tell you from my own experience that having a self-published book on Amazon is a great credibility builder. People automatically perceive you as an expert in your field when they see that you have written a book. I have been very fortunate with the books that I have written. I can tell you for certain that it has produced many opportunities for me. They are great door openers. As they say in the self-publishing business, "You make more money explaining your book than on your book." Essentially, it is really a door opener and allows you to grab the attention of groups, organizations, and individuals that you can potentially do business with.

As I mentioned earlier, I would also strongly suggest that you become proficient at speaking in public. For many, this is a terrifying prospect. It needn't be. There are too many benefits to derive from learning how to speak in public to not do it. First and foremost, it separates you from the crowd. Once again, people perceive you as an expert if you get up in front of them and talk about your field of expertise.

One of the best ways I know to learn to get comfortable and good at public speaking is to join Toastmasters International. It wasn't until I was in my early 30s that I decided to join a local Toastmasters group. That came about because of an incident I had speaking in front of about 75 people in a college class I attended. I was terrified of the prospect of speaking in public. The teacher had told us that we had to do a presentation in front of the class as a big part of our grade. I ended up being one of the last people to speak that day and had worked myself up into a nervous wreck by the time I got up to speak. The heat in the room was turned up high, and I was beginning to sweat like a farm animal. By the time my talk was finished, I was wringing wet and looked like I just crossed the finish line at the Boston Marathon. To make matters worse, the teacher asked me to help him pass out some papers after my talk. I thought of it as "punishment" for being so ridiculously nervous. It was a humiliating experience I swore I'd never put myself through again.

I told someone I knew about the experience and they told me I should join Toastmasters. They said it helped them tremendously. I had never heard of it before, but I decided I would check it out.

Little did I know the many benefits that I would derive from joining the group in learning how to speak in public. I can't think of any other setting where you can learn this important skill. Everybody is there for the same purpose, to support others who are wanting to become proficient at public speaking. I only wish I would've discovered this earlier in my life and career. Speaking in public is just one of the many benefits you'll derive from joining Toastmasters. You'll also become a better listener, be much more confident in your daily life, and learn how to think on your feet and respond quickly and cogently.

The amazing thing about Toastmasters is that it teaches you to overcome your fears and get outside your comfort zone. As the saying goes, "Life begins outside your comfort zone."

I've seen some amazing transformations of personalities at Toastmasters. I've seen timid people go from being frozen in terror and unable to speak in front of a group, to being proficient public speakers and giving wonderful talks in front of others within six months. To watch them turn from these meek individuals into outgoing personalities who can light up a room is quite amazing.

That confidence spills into so many other areas in your life that it's hard to comprehend. The beautiful thing about getting outside your comfort zone is that each time you do, the next time becomes a little bit easier. There is a scientific reason behind it; we are wired in such a way that until we expose ourselves to those situations that make us uncomfortable, we remain fearful. Once we allow ourselves to experience them over and over again, confronting those fears and self-limiting mental barriers, our fears and worries diminish. As the old saying goes, "Face your fears and your fears will disappear."

Do yourself a huge favor and contact Toastmasters International to find out where some of the local Toastmasters clubs are located in your area. Then, attend a few of their meetings in the different clubs in your area to find out which ones seem to resonate with you most. Once you find one that feels more like home, then join them and give it a try for a while. You will find it to be one of the best things you could do for both your personal and professional life. I promise you, you'll be glad you made that decision. It's a major game changer.

I want to tell you a quick story about how my experience at Toastmasters early on made a significant difference in my professional life. About seven or eight months after I joined Toastmasters, I was working on a transaction with a partner on renewing a Bank of America branch lease. About midway through the transaction, the corporate real estate person we were dealing with left the company for health reasons. The person who ran the corporate real estate department we were dealing with took over. After working with her on the assignment for a couple of months she asked us if we would be willing to give a seminar to all the people in the corporate real estate department, of which there were about 30. When I first heard this, pure terror ran through my veins. Then, I realized it was a huge opportunity to get in front of all of the corporate real estate people who were running the bank's transactions in our area. I told her we would be happy to. She gave us 30 days to put the seminar together. It was a full day seminar, and we ended up getting to know all of the various corporate real estate people at that location. We also received seven new assignments from some of the people whom we met there and more assignments later from some of the others who attended the seminar. This never would've happened had I said no to her request or had not been attending Toastmasters, which gave me the courage to take advantage of the opportunity. This is only one of the benefits I initially received from joining. Many more benefits have been derived over the years for which I will always be grateful.

Action Items

⮞ Take courses, subscribe to podcasts, and read some books about marketing with the objective of becoming an expert marketer

⮞ Start writing articles on your field of expertise. If you write one article per month, after one year, you will have 12 articles to create an eBook

⮞ Become proficient at public speaking by joining a local Toastmasters club

⮞ Challenge yourself and get used to getting out of your comfort zone regularly. You'll be amazed at the results. "Life begins outside your comfort zone."

CHAPTER 11

Success Stories of Agents Who Work Both Residential and Commercial Real Estate Brokerage

"Everything you've ever wanted is on
the other side of fear."
~ *George Addair*

I've had the pleasure of meeting and getting to know several successful residential agents who do both sides of the real estate business. I have also met several successful agents that started out doing residential exclusively and made the move over to commercial real estate full-time.

I asked a couple of them to share their stories to help others see what challenges and successes they had to go through. I believe their stories will give you a much clearer picture of what it takes and how to make it work for yourself.

I'll start out with David Hyun. David has some impressive credentials and a background in architecture, engineering, planning, and construction. He decided he would go into the residential end of the business. He worked at it for a couple years and did not do all that well. He always had an interest in the commercial end of the business, so he made the transition into commercial. His family owned some commercial income properties, and he liked working with the numbers on it. It seemed to come more naturally to him and best suited his strengths. He ended up making the right move and even received the prestigious National Association of Realtors, 2016 National Commercial Awards.

Here are some of David's recommendations:

- Work as an assistant for a reputable commercial broker to learn the ropes.
- It can take a few years to get proficient at it, so be patient.
- It takes long hours and you should be physically fit to handle it.
- Knowledge is power in the commercial real estate business.
- Join your local CCIM Chapter and get to know the successful brokers since they will be the ones giving you helpful advice.

David is a consummate professional. He speaks elegantly and is good at what he does because he works toward being the best at it.

The next person I'd like to tell you about is Greg Palazzo. He's a sharp guy who works hard and is very service oriented. He's also successful and the type of agent you'd want to handle your side of the transaction. Greg started out on the residential side and gradually made his way into commercial. I asked him about his decision process for moving into the commercial side.

- What made you decide to start doing commercial transactions after you had been in the residential real estate business?

GREG: It's kind of a long story; it wasn't an overnight decision. Here's the short version: I'd been interested in the "commercial" side of real estate ever since receiving my license in 1995, but at the time, it seemed too confusing and exclusive. I didn't know anybody in the industry or even where to start. Truthfully, I wasn't ready for any type of real estate sales until 2003 when a large builder hired me on. In 2007, I moved on to become a residential realtor.

Eventually, I signed on with a residential broker who challenged me to "just do it" after I mentioned to him my continuing curiosity regarding commercial real estate sales. Nobody in our office was active in the commercial real estate business. Then one day, a floor call was transferred to me from my broker. It was an investor group looking to buy the old City Center Motel in Ventura, CA. The investor group called our firm randomly because the listing broker didn't return their sign call fast enough, or so they said.

Anyhow, they said that they were purchasing motels close to the ocean along the coast of California and they happened to be in Ventura for their next purchase. They asked me if I could represent them and write an offer. I told them the truth about my lack of experience and that I never did anything with commercial. I even told them that my goal is to eventually be a full time commercial agent. I was amazed when they said that that it was "no problem" and "they would walk me through the process"! I told my broker what just happened, and of course, he said, "yeah, just do it." So, I wrote the entire offer with my new investor client's guidance, and we submitted the offer.

That deal got me excited about the commercial real estate business. Sadly, it took me another six years to fully take the plunge as a full time commercial broker.

• What is it that you liked about doing both commercial and residential real estate?

GREG: I'm a full time commercial broker now. What I really like about commercial is that, for the most part, there are far fewer emotional swings within the decision-making process. With residential, I did enjoy the emotion after closing escrow and witnessing elated customers.

• What would you say is the most challenging part of doing both residential and commercial real estate transactions?

GREG: The most challenging part of residential was dealing with some of my customers' emotional highs and lows.

The most challenging part of commercial is gaining product knowledge, learning different zone codes for each city, parking requirements, types of leases, etc.

- What would you recommend to residential real estate agents who are interested working on commercial real estate transactions and looking to get started?

GREG: Make sure that you have some money saved and/or a supplemental income during your learning process. Don't do it "part-time." Sign on with a commercial brokerage firm that has a good reputation, quality training, and mentoring.

- Do you have any favorite or memorable transactions you have done when you first started out doing commercial?

GREG: There are a few. The City Center Motel proposal in Ventura was memorable. That wasn't my favorite though. My colleague and I sold an industrial building in Camarillo, CA. The day we interviewed to get the listing, the owner told us that he and his wife both just found out that they each had cancer. Three months later she passed away. The day after closing escrow he passed away. That was about one year after his wife's passing. He was so grateful that we sold his building prior to his passing. I'm proud to have been included on that transaction.

- What's the best advice you can give to a residential agent who is interested in working on commercial transactions?

GREG: Figure out one or two specific types of commercial real estate that you want to specialize in. Not all commercial real estate is the same. Learn the due diligence process for your specialty. Be well prepared and don't compare commercial to residential.

I have found that the agents I have interviewed about their experience in working their way into the commercial side of the business all have some common themes.

Here are the ones I heard continuously:

- Be a non-stop learner of what you want and need to know about commercial transactions.
- Get around successful commercial agents and be a "sponge" for all the advice and help they offer you.

I speak regularly at various residential and commercial brokerage companies, as well as Board of Realtors locations in the Los Angeles area.

Here are a few common questions I get regularly:

- What types of commercial properties should I start with?

    Start with the type of commercial property you're interested in. If you have no interest in a specific type of commercial property, then start with the first lead you get for a commercial property requirement and then find someone who is knowledgeable with that type of property to help you. It's best to start studying the various aspects of commercial properties prior to "jumping in," so you have some familiarity.

- How long does it take to move into commercial real estate full-time?

    That depends on your ability to start generating business on the commercial side. I tell newcomers who are starting out as "runners," the first year is basically "grad school," when you're learning how things work and what needs to be done. You can make money, but you must be prepared to "hang in there" for at least a year before your pipeline is lined up and paying you enough to keep going. In other words, have some money saved up to carry you while you're learning. Residential transactions have a shorter pay-off timeframe. The commercial transactions can happen faster, but it's not the typical duration of deal flows. There are more moving parts, and the transactions are more complex and require legal counsel to review many times; then, there are other factors that will come into play, such as environmental reports, seismic reports, geologic reports, etc. These all take time.

• What do you have to do to become proficient at commercial real estate transactions and how long does it take?

Like any other skill you're trying to learn and become proficient at, it takes time and patience, as well as perseverance. It's not "rocket science," but you need to spend the time and energy to learn the fundamentals and the nuances of it. One of my favorite sayings is from James Allen's *As a Man Thinketh*: "The strength of the effort is the measure of the result." Apply that mindset to anything you're trying to learn or acquire in life. It can take 3-5 years to start feeling like you're getting proficient, depending on how many transactions you're handling. It can happen faster. Like any other skill it takes years to master. Stay at it, and you'll get there.

CHAPTER 12

How Tenants May Structure Commercial Leases

"Build your own dreams, or someone else
will hire you to build theirs."
~ *Farrah Gray*

If you're looking to help tenants find lease space and help them negotiate favorable terms for their lease, then you'll need to become familiar with the terminology and salient terms involved with leasing that can impact your client's lease obligation.

I certainly can't give you all the details of commercial leasing here in this chapter. The intent is to give you a base foundation under which you can build upon your knowledge in leasing commercial space. You have acquired some of it already, which we covered in the previous chapter. My hope is to give you some more detail, so you know what you're doing when discussing leasing with a prospective client. Finding and leasing them commercial space while representing their best interests is paramount in your communication and intent with them.

First, get familiar with leasing terminology, especially for the type of lease you're going to be trying to locate and negotiate for your client. Read a sample lease form for the genre type of lease space your client needs and learn the lease terms. You can find a Glossary of Real Estate Terms and various forms and lease samples on my website at www.impactcoachingsystems.com.

Let's review some salient lease terms

Base Rent: A set amount used as a minimum rent with provisions for increasing the rent over the term of the lease.

Base rent can be increased throughout the term of the lease annually with a fixed amount or percentage such as 3% per annum; also, it can be negotiated for increases every two years, or midway through the term, or whatever the tenant and landlord may agree to.

Rental Concessions: Depending upon the rental market, economy, supply and demand, lease term, credit-worthiness of the tenant, and the landlord's desire to get the space leased, a tenant may be able to get concessions from the landlord to induce them to sign a lease. Many times, this will include free rent for a period, beneficial occupancy, meaning no rent paid for a period of time while the tenant prepares the lease space for their tenancy, which is common with retail space, additional tenant improvement dollars contributed to the tenant by the landlord, moving allowance, or any number of enticements that the landlord is willing to give them. These "concessions" are usually not available to tenants in a tight market where there's little space available or high demand. You will see concessions freely given in down markets where there are plentiful choices for tenants and motivated landlords abound.

Effective Rent vs. Face Rent: The face rent is the rent stated on the lease that the tenant is obligated to pay. The effective rent is the actual dollar amount that the landlord receives after concessions of free rent are factored in.

For example: The lease states that the tenant must pay $2.00/sf/mo. Or $24/sf/yr. rent. The tenant signs a five-year lease. In order to entice the tenant to sign the lease for five years the landlord offers to give them six months' rent at no charge, as follows: months 2 and 3 are free, and months 13, 24, 36, and 48 are free during the initial lease term. The six months of free base rent are equal to 10% of the sixty-month term. So, the tenant is receiving a 10% discount, or $24.00 face rental rate minus $2.40= $21.60/sf effective rental rate.

If you're the landlord and want to preserve the value of the building, you would want to get the tenant to sign a 66-month lease term. That way you aren't lowering the value of the lease because you're discounting the rent outside the lease term. This is important if the landlord is planning on selling the property or re-financing it. It's also a way to increase the building's value by getting a higher face rate when giving free rent inside the lease term. As long as the tenant is okay with doing that and can afford the higher rent when the free rent burns off, it can be a 'win-win' for everyone. Beware though because the higher rent is sometimes more than some tenants can really afford after they have the 'rent holiday' of paying nothing for a while. I'm a big believer in spreading it out in increments of half rent. For example, six months free rent can be spread out as half rent months 2-13. That way the tenant can have a longer period to get the business going, pay for new furnishings, etc. The landlord is still getting some rent instead of nothing for a period of time, so it can be a 'win-win' scenario.

Other issues with which you can help your client as a tenant representative include getting other professionals involved with the process to guide them through their move. These may include architectural/space planners, tenant improvement contractors, moving companies, design consultants, and any specialty contractors or vendors that are specific to their needs, such as restaurant suppliers, retail fixture vendors, etc.

The idea is to build a network of professionals that can help to make your clients' moves easier for them, while watching out for their best interests. The good news is that once you have a network in place, they can help you with referrals.

I can't emphasize the importance enough of having a competent real estate attorney guiding your clients through the leasing process of negotiating their lease. Many times, I've come across owners and tenants who hired their corporate or estate attorney to negotiate leases for them only to put them at a major disadvantage because their attorney didn't know what they were doing when it came time to negotiate their lease.

Operating Expenses: Depending upon the lease type, use, building, landlord, and other factors like negotiations, operating expenses can be a big portion of a tenant's lease expenses. You'll want to determine as best as possible what those are and which ones the tenant will be responsible for.

For example, if it's a retail or industrial lease, the tenant will generally be responsible for their pro rata share of much of the property's expenses. Office properties, explained earlier, are generally full service gross leases, with the landlord responsible for most expenses and the tenant being responsible for their pro rata share for any overage amount, over and above the base year amount. On a modified-gross basis the tenant will pay for electrical or electrical and janitorial.

There are variations on all of these. You will get familiar with your region's standards by speaking with other agents and landlords.

One thing you want to keep in mind is when negotiating a lease, try to put a cap on expenses and make sure that there are exclusions of certain types of operating expenses. I don't want to go into a full discussion of those here. If your client has a good real estate attorney, they will have a list of operating expense exclusions they will submit to the landlord. Smaller tenants, i.e. under 3,000sf have less leverage than larger ones. Your ability to get any exclusions depends on the landlord and building size. It's always worth asking for. Remember the old saying, "If you don't ask, the answer is always no."

I don't want you to think you're going to learn all about leasing commercial space in this book. There are many good books available to do that. Hopefully, I've given you a basis of how commercial leases can be structured and how you may be able to assist someone who is looking to lease space.

I urge you to read up and study about commercial leasing and get more familiar with how they can be structured.

Action Items

➡ Start familiarizing yourself with the lease jargon and lease forms. You can find some at our website: www.impactcoachingsystems.com.

➡ Purchase my book, *The How to Add Value Handbook for Commercial Real Estate,* which will give you a good foundation with leasing.

➡ Purchase other books and audiobooks pertaining to leasing.

➡ "Remember no one can make you feel inferior without your consent." –Eleanor Roosevelt

CHAPTER 13

20 Things You Can Do to Fast Track Your Commercial Real Estate Earnings

1. Order the top five commercial real estate books on Amazon.
2. Join Audible.com and order the top five audiobooks on commercial real estate that are different from the books that you ordered (If you play them at 1.5x speed you can listen to more audiobooks faster and still understand and enjoy them) Listen to audiobooks constantly while driving. You'll be turning drive-time into learning-time. Talk radio and music are just "chewing gum" for the mind. It's okay to listen to occasionally, but not all the time.
3. Subscribe to the top five podcasts on commercial real estate. There are many good ones and new ones being added all the time. Find the ones that you enjoy and resonate with.
4. Sign up for at least three video training courses on commercial real estate in the next six months (you can start with mine if you want to have an edge on your competition by having a Unique Selling Proposition at: impactcoachingsystems.com/courses).
5. Commit to studying at least one hour per day in commercial real estate subjects.
6. Pick a submarket in your town or city where you can become familiar with commercial real estate values in both sales and leasing.
7. Pick a property type you want to start becoming an expert in around your city or town and make it your business to become familiar with those properties and their owners.

8. Check with your local community college or university for extension courses in commercial real estate and find one you can sign up for and attend.

9. Look at and sign up for Mike Lipsey's courses on commercial real estate at www.lipseyco.com or check out some of the other ones out there such as on Udemy or other platforms.

10. Learn who the commercial real estate brokers are in your area and introduce yourself to them and call the local commercial brokerage firms in your area. Ask for the listing secretary and then request that you be put on their list of brokers to receive the office listings both for sale and lease.

11. Look into becoming a Certified Commercial Investment Member (CCIM) and check out the courses they offer. They are top-notch courses that will make you stand out amongst your peers.

12. Start attending meetings that are offered by Building Owners & Managers Association (BOMA) or Institute of Real Estate Management (IREM).

13. If you are in a real estate brokerage office that has both residential and commercial brokers, find a commercial agent you can partner up with who understands and works the commercial side while you're first starting out.

14. Be sure to take some commercial real estate investment financial analysis courses either online or at your local college.

15. Learn the basics of commercial leases and lease terminology.

16. Become familiar with purchase and sale agreements for commercial properties. You can find sample forms, leases, lease proposals and other valuable forms on my website under the Resources tab at: www.impactcoachingsystems.com.

17. Once you are comfortable with your basic understanding and knowledge of commercial real estate values and terminology, start soliciting business from your contacts to get started.

18. Become proficient at conducting due diligence when helping others to purchase investment properties. This will set you apart from the majority of other agents out there who work investments.

19. If you really want to supercharge your career, then join Toastmasters International, where you not only learn how to speak in front of others, but you will also gain a whole other level of self-confidence you never knew. It has helped me tremendously not only in my career but in my personal life as well. I highly recommend it to anyone who is serious about taking their career to a higher level.

20. Study and learn all you can about marketing. Now, more than ever, it is extremely important for you to become proficient at selling yourself and your services, as well as the products you represent. By learning how to market and write well, you will place yourself way above your competition.

In Conclusion

The world around us is changing faster than ever and seems to be picking up more speed every day. If we are to be able to keep up with the needs and service requirements of our existing and prospective clients and customers, we need to be constantly working on getting better and more proficient at what we do to serve others. That means learning new skills to better serve them, becoming more effective communicators, becoming better marketers, and becoming more proficient in all areas of our lives all while trying to maintain a balance of our priorities. It sounds daunting, and it can be, but you can do it if you are disciplined and focused.

Today's world demands that all of us be more flexible and willing to change course when necessary, adapt to keep moving forward, and try being the best at what we do. If you're not getting better, you're going backwards.

I don't know about you, but I sure feel as though I'm "pushing a boulder up a hill" sometimes. You must stay committed to constant and never-ending improvement in all the various areas of life. That doesn't mean we'll be perfect at it or that everything will be running great all the time. You must be resilient and willing to pick yourself up if you take a fall and forgive yourself, as well as others, when things aren't working out. That's what makes "champions" out of us, doing the things that others are unwilling to do, to become masters of our craft. That has always been the case throughout history. It's more critical now more than ever.

I read a great quote by Les Brown, the famous motivational speaker, who said, "Most people will not participate in their own rescue." All we need to do is look around at those who have not adapted or are unwilling to accept, adapt and be flexible to our changing world. You know who they are. Don't be one of those examples. Be the kind of example that others talk about and say, "she is the type of person that makes circumstances work out for her," or "he's the type of person who figures out what needs to be done and then does it."

There are more opportunities out there in the world today than at any time in human history. We need only look for and put them to work.

I'll leave you with this:

Find a way to serve others by serving God. We're here to love and serve. All the world's saints and sages have told us that throughout history.

One of my favorite sayings is from Paramahansa Yogananda, author of the spiritual classic *"Autobiography of a Yogi"*:

"Remain calm; do your best; leave the rest to God.

That is all He expects."

If you keep service to God and loving others foremost in your mind, there's no way you will not be successful. He is the "Giver of all Gifts." You will be amazed how life will turn out. I'm speaking from experience.

I want to thank you for purchasing and reading my book. If you found it to be helpful, I'd like to ask a favor of you. I would greatly appreciate it if you would please leave a review on Amazon for me. It helps to spur Amazon to make further efforts to promote it.

I encourage you to download the audiobook and listen to it periodically to remind yourself of some of the key fundamentals, ideas, and strategies that can be used to help keep the skills you've learned at the top of your mind. It also further embeds the information in your psyche, allowing recall of it more easily.

Remember, you will also find some helpful information and downloadable forms that are useful at my website. These include the Competitive Lease and Building Comparable sheets, sample leases, sample credit report authorization forms, sample tenant applications, and other useful forms that you will want to use during your leasing and investment activity.

In addition, I'd love to get your feedback on the books, audiobooks, and video courses on my website at www.impactcoachingsystems.com. It's always welcomed and appreciated.

Wishing you all the best –

Brian Hennessey

Acknowledgments

First and foremost, I thank God for all that I have in my life. For all the many blessings I'm aware of and unaware of. He is the Giver of ALL Gifts. I know all good comes from Him, and I'm eternally grateful for all He's given me. We need only to become more aware and conscious of all the prayers and desires He has granted us in our lives to see Him working in it always.

There were many people who helped me along the way in my career that I'd love to mention, but there's not room enough to put all their names in here. My heartfelt thanks to all of those from whom I've learned much. I know they know who they are.

To all my friends and colleagues who helped me with this endeavor, I thank you all for the valuable input you had and shared with me for this book. Your help is appreciated more than words can express.

Love to all of you –

Sample Letter Agreements and Forms

Exclusive Right to Represent for Purchase

Date

NAME
COMPANY
STREET ADDRESS
CITY, STATE, ZIP

RE: [Subject Property Address]

Dear _____,

Please allow this letter to confirm our understanding regarding the acquisition of the above referenced property.

This letter confirms that you have become aware of the potential availability of this property through (insert agent's name and company) and authorizes me as the procuring cause, to represent [INDIVIDUAL/COMPANY NAME] and its related entities in the potential purchase, ground lease, joint venture, or transfer of ownership of this real estate asset.

It is further understood that the Buyer and/or its related entities shall pay me the commission based upon _____ percent (_%) of the total sales price at the close of escrow in cash.

This agreement shall remain in full force and effect for a period of one (1) year from the date of this agreement and is to be construed in accordance with and governed by the laws of the State of _____. In the event that it becomes necessary to settle a dispute regarding the Agreement through litigation, the prevailing party shall be entitled to its actual attorney's fees and costs from the opposing party as determined by the court.

Please sign and date below, acknowledging the agreement.

Sincerely,
[Company Name]
[Agent's name]

Agreed and accepted:

_____   Date_____

Exclusive Right to Lease or Purchase

Date

NAME OF CLIENT
COMPANY NAME (IF APPLICABLE)
ADDRESS CITY, STATE, ZIP CODE

RE: Exclusive Right to Represent

Dear _____,

You hereby appoint [your name] as sole broker and grant me the exclusive right to obtain a lease or purchase of premises on our behalf, commencing on the date of this agreement until [expiration date].

I will enlist my best efforts and those of my firm to secure a location satisfactory to you, and if I deem it necessary, I will also solicit the cooperation of other real estate brokers. You will refer to me all inquiries and offerings received by you and all negotiations shall be conducted solely by you or under your direction, subject to your final approval.

I will acquire the details on all contemplated or presently available locations and carefully select and present to you, at a time convenient to you, those which in your opinion are the most suitable for your occupancy. If and when you decide on a location, I will negotiate the terms of the purchase or lease on your behalf and in your interest, taking advantage of my knowledge of real estate values and rentals and terms of the numerous sales and leases previously negotiated by our firm.

If, for any reason, you are dissatisfied with the level of service I am providing us during the term of this agreement, you reserve the right to terminate it with written notification to me of such termination.

Unless otherwise agreed, I will look only to the landlord or seller, as the situation may be, for my commission or fee. Subsequent to the termination of this agreement, you shall continue to recognize me as your exclusive broker in accordance with the terms hereof, with respect to any prospective locations or owners which I have submitted to you during the term of this agreement.

Sincerely,

[Your Company Name]

By: _____
          (Your name)

Agreed: _____   _____
          (Authorized signatory)   Date

COMPETITIVE SET BUILDING COMPARABLE SHEET

Broker(s)	Building Name	Address	Comments	Owners	# of Stories	Building Size (SF)	Site Area (Acre)	Year Built	% Occupied	Average In-place Rent	Asking Rental Rate	Concessions Offered	Major Tenant(s)	Parking Ratio	Parking Rates
Colliers Int'l	Summit Building	1234 Mt. Olympus Dr.	Newer building with LEED status. Class 'A' steel and concrete	Zeus & Co.	140,000	6	5 acres	2015	92.0%	$36.00	$ 40.00	1 month free rent per year of lease term	Aphrodite Insurance	5/1000	$85/mo.

COMPETITIVE SET LEASE COMPARABLES

Date Exec	Tenant	Address	City	Size	Term	Ask Rate	Face Rate	Lease Type	Tenant Improvement Allowance	Comments

*These and other valuable forms can be found
at our website at www.impactcoachingsystems.com*

Consulting Services

Brian offers his consulting services on creating value, facilitating cash flow, and navigating the due diligence process for individuals and groups. He will teach you the necessary skills to gain a greater understanding of how to conduct a thorough investigation of commercial real estate investments for acquisition. Once these strategies and principles have been learned and incorporated into your skillset, you will have them for life to reduce your risk or your client's risk of making a bad investment and help to create greater value.

Here are a few of the ways his consulting services can be structured:

1. **One-on-one instruction**— He will work with you one-on-one to teach you the step-by-step instructions for conducting a thorough and proper "deep dive" due diligence investigation. You can custom design a program with him to correlate with your specific interests, or you can use a pre-designed general program that he provides his consulting clients.

2. **Have Brian Conduct Due Diligence on a Property**— Hire Brian to conduct the actual due diligence process and teach you and your team as he goes through the process, so you can learn as he goes through the transaction with you.

3. **Team Instruction**— Have you and your team learn all the details and instructions to incorporate into your acquisition process. This will allow each team member to know all the necessary steps and their respective role when conducting due diligence. Once your team has these skills in their tool set they will perform like a well-oiled machine and will be less likely to miss important items and issues or let things fall through the cracks.

4. **Specific Issues and Concerns Needed to be Addressed—** Hire Brian to discuss only specific issues and concerns you need help with as needed.

   • "Deep Dive" Consultation—Spend the day with Brian— You can spend the day with Brian and ask him all the questions you'd like, learn all you can from him about some specific transactions, or work however you want to structure it.

Please contact Brian Hennessey to discuss rates and how you may be able to customize a program that best suits you and your needs. He can be reached at 818.371.0311 or brian@impactcoachingsystems.com

Resources

Recommended websites, educational programs, books, audiobooks and podcasts

Websites

CoStar.com and LoopNet.com

CoStar.com and LoopNet.com (owned by CoStar) are some of the most heavily trafficked commercial real estate websites. CoStar is where passion, creativity, and a drive for results come together to influence the way the $17 trillion commercial real estate industry does business. Their suite of online services enables clients to analyze, interpret and gain unmatched insight on commercial property values, market conditions and current availabilities.

CREXI

Commercial Real Estate Exchange, Inc. (CREXi) is the commercial real estate industry's fastest growing marketplace and technology platform dedicated to supporting the CRE industry and its stakeholders. CREXi enables commercial real estate professionals to quickly streamline, manage, and grow their businesses using the industry's most advanced transaction management solution.

Showcase.com

Tenants and investors can search here, and commercial agents can advertise their properties or lease space.

Commercialcafe.com

Commercial Café is a listings and data provider offering a suite of products and services to professionals in the commercial real estate industry. Use the platform to add, search or compare office, retail, and industrial listings for lease or for sale, get data on off-market properties, and lease space online.

Google Earth
A "must have" for anyone who is looking at properties for investment. Why drive there first, when you can first look with a "bird's eye" view of the property? Download it and have it on your desktop for easy access.

Officespace.com
Specializes in all types of office space, including large scale space, smaller offices for independent businesses and coworking spaces. The site has listings in most major US cities, and users can search by city or state.

Keyvon.com
Your source for commercial property values. Use Keyvon Value to get your commercial property values specific to your location. Register for free and get information specific to buildings. This is not meant to replace appraisals or expert opinion from licensed professionals.

Multifamilyinsiders.com
This site is all about apartments including management, trends, investment, leasing, etc.

Books
- *You Can Negotiate Anything* by Herb Cohen
- *Getting More: How You Can Negotiate to Succeed in Work and Life* by Stuart Diamond
- *Secrets of Power Negotiating* by Roger Dawson
- *Getting to Yes* by Roger Fisher and William Ury
- *Influence: The Psychology of Persuasion* by Robert Cialdini
- *Confessions of a Real Estate Entrepreneur* by James A. Randel
- *The Complete Guide to Buying and Selling Apartment Buildings* by Steve Berges
- *What Every Real Estate Investor Needs to Know About Cash Flow* by Frank Gallenelli

Software

Argussoftware.com
Argus products have become the industry standard and provide the complete solution for transacting, managing and growing your commercial real estate portfolio. This software is sophisticated and requires comprehensive training. Financial institutions will generally want to see an Argus financial run on bigger properties so they can manipulate the assumptions within the financial analysis to comply with their underwriting guidelines. This software goes beyond the needs of the average commercial real estate investor.

Realdata.com
Analyze commercial and industrial leases easily and accurately using Real Data's Comparative Lease Analysis software. Just enter the terms and conditions in the fill-in-the-blanks program and in minutes you can compare the true cost or benefit of up to six scenarios.

Procalc.com
This is the industry standard lease analysis software program currently used by thousands of commercial real estate professionals. It is an excellent program for owners/landlords, brokers, property and asset managers, and offers customer service second to none.

Financial Analyst/ Argus Software Specialist
Wayne Edmondson can be reached at 714.734.0162
Or wayne.edmondson@gmail.com
Wayne is one of the best financial analysts I've ever had the privilege to work with. He knows Argus backwards and forward. He is your 'go-to' guy if you need an Argus financial analysis for an investment property or portfolio of properties.

Glossary of Real Estate Terms

The Glossary of Real Estate Terms can be found at our website at: www.impactcoachingsystems.com. You'll also find several useful forms for your commercial real estate business as well as sample proposals and lease forms under the Resources tab.

Podcasts

- *Best Real Estate Investing Advice Ever* with Joe Fairless
- *Old Dawg's REI Network Real Estate Investing for Seniors* with Bill Manassero
- *Real Estate Investing for Cash Flow* with Kevin Bupp
- *Apartment Building Investing* with Michael Blank
- *Creating Wealth Real Estate Investing* with Jason Hartman

About the Author

Brian Hennessey has been in the commercial real estate industry for 30+ years as: a commercial broker; a Senior Vice President of Acquisitions/ Dispositions and also ran his own real estate syndication/asset management company. He has represented a number of Fortune 500 Tenants including: Bank of America, The Walt Disney Company and Baxter Healthcare. With over 12 million square feet of sale and lease transactions; some of which were with some of the largest Owner/Landlords in the country. Brian has accumulated a wealth of experience.

The Due Diligence Handbook for Commercial Real Estate, a #1 Bestseller on Amazon in Commercial Real Estate books, was written originally as a personal reference tool/checklist because of the many facets and the volume of information that is needed to be remembered for each transaction. He also is the author of the *The How to Add Value Handbook for Commercial Real Estate.* Both are also available as audiobooks on Audible.com and iTunes.

He shares his experiences, strategies, tactics, and the many lessons learned over the years as an acquisition executive, investor, and commercial real estate broker. He enjoys training others about how to properly conduct the due diligence process when purchasing investment properties. He believes it helps to raise the bar and standards for those professionals who assist others in buying commercial properties so they may become more valuable team members and true allies to their clients.

You can find out more information on his seminars and other training materials at www.impactcoachingsystems.com. You can reach him at brian@impactcoachingsystems.com.

The Due Diligence Handbook for Commercial Real Estate

by Brian Hennessey

Available on Amazon: #1 Best Seller and consistently rated in the top commercial real estate books on Amazon.com

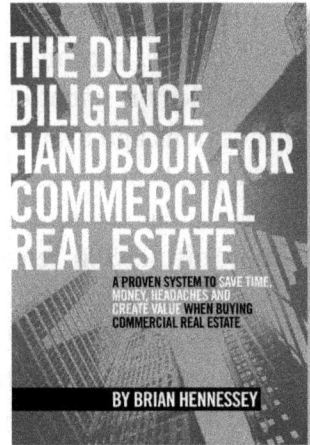

There's a huge problem in the commercial real estate business that nobody is talking about—DUE DILIGENCE. The vast majority of investors, real estate brokers and commercial real estate professionals barely scratch the surface conducting their due diligence when purchasing commercial real estate investments. Investors are taking unnecessary risks and throwing money away or making bad investments, by not properly performing due diligence. Brokers are putting themselves at risk for potential litigation and missing an opportunity to help their clients as a true ally by learning these principles.

Having and adhering to a proven system keeps you from missing something and allows you to do it faster, easier and more efficiently.

Some of the things you will learn:

- What to negotiate in the purchase and sale agreement so that you can maximize the opportunities for yourself when it comes time to negotiate further with the seller
- How to properly review leases so that you know what to look for that could be cause for concern
- How to choose a lender or mortgage broker
- Third party reports, such as Environmental; Property Condition Assessment; Seismic/PML; Geologic and

other reports that a lender may require and what to look for in them

- Tips on how to negotiate loan terms and specific provisions in them so you can avoid getting burned later
- Conducting tenant interviews and what questions to ask them so that you can uncover any problems or issues that you would otherwise not be made aware of (Super Powerful. Must learn or you'll miss out.)
- Cost cutting tips and strategies that will help you add value to the property once you own it
- What to look for when reviewing books and records and what to ask the seller for
- One of the most critical processes done during the due diligence process is the underwriting and financial analysis, which is constantly being revised during that process. In the book, there is a list of questions that must be addressed and answered while adjusting your financial analysis of the investment and will help you to more accurately assess the potential of how the numbers should work
- How to deal with the appraiser and appraisal process to be more proactive and enhance the potential for the highest possible loan amount
- How to ensure that you are getting everything you deserve when finalizing the transaction and what to look for on the closing statement that may be added by the seller or lender as a credit to them, that you can get eliminated or at least negotiated down by being aware of what to look for

In addition, you get at the end of the book:

- A Sample Lease Abstract Form (which shows you how to fill in all the salient deal points and provisions of a lease document)

- Due Diligence Checklist (an essential list of most all items of which you should ask a seller for when negotiating a purchase)
- Due Diligence Document Checklist (an essential list of most all the documents you should request from a seller when negotiating a purchase)
- Sample Tenant Questionnaire (a sample list of questions that you should ask of tenants when conducting a tenant interview)

The book has become successful beyond my wildest dreams and has started a movement of awareness for investors that is very gratifying. I realized this after receiving many emails from around the world telling me how much the information helped them in acquiring investment properties by keeping them from making costly mistakes and creating value for them. It is also is fast becoming a disruptor in the commercial brokerage industry, as it raises the awareness of the need for brokers to become more involved in helping their clients with due diligence when helping them buy investment property.

Comments from some of the readers of *The Due Diligence Handbook for Commercial Real Estate:*

Thorough and thoughtful due diligence
benefits everyone involved

Investors gain confidence, reduce expenses and avoid mistakes. ... At the end of the day, a sound due diligence process creates tremendous value for everyone involved. ... With this book, Brian Hennessey has encapsulated lessons from decades of experience in nearly every facet of the commercial real estate business. The result is an invaluable resource for reducing risk, maximizing value and accelerating the process of due diligence in commercial real estate transactions. This book is a great tool that will allow both clients and professionals to leave the office earlier and sleep better at night.

~ Doug Frye, President and CEO,
Global, Colliers International

Must Read if you are buying any commercial property

The author has done a great job identifying the items and issues that must be reviewed and considered before purchasing an investment property. The book takes a step by step approach and is very comprehensive. It provides good check lists and forms, and identifies many due diligence items that most people would not think of. I run a real estate investment company and would recommend this book to anyone who is considering buying an investment property.

~ Mike Adler, President,
Adler Realty Investments

Investigate Investment Real Estate
Like a Seasoned Professional

What a helpful tool for anyone (including old pros) acquiring commercial real estate. Too many investors find trouble only after they have closed escrow. However, many after closing issues can be avoided with a thorough due diligence review prior to owning. Mr. Hennessey has provided a thorough overview of the items an investor should investigate. If the advice offered in this book is followed completely, even the most unsophisticated first-time buyer will appear to be a seasoned commercial acquisition expert.

~ Bruce Blumenthal, V.P. Acquisitions,
Blue Ridge Properties

The How to Add Value Handbook for Commercial Real Estate

by Brian Hennessey

Available on Amazon

Quit running your investment property under the influence of "hopeium"; that delusional state under which you believe everything will work out fine without putting forth any effort or thought into creating value with it. That's the way most investors approach their investment property management plan.

Without a strategy for increasing value with your property's management plan is just taking the "lottery" approach.

You want the "Cliff Notes" version. In other words, the 20% that will give you 80% of the results, and not a bunch of minutia with 30 to 50 pages of fluff that you have to sift through to find the helpful tips or key points.

The fundamentals remain the same for the most part, when it comes to adding value and leasing. This information can be used across the various genres of commercial real estate investments, whether it's office and industrial, retail or multi-family residential properties. I comment from time to time throughout the book on the different angles or strategies you may want to consider for the different property types, which I have obtained from my own background and experience of 30+ years in the commercial real estate industry--or from those I know to be the best at their particular specialty.

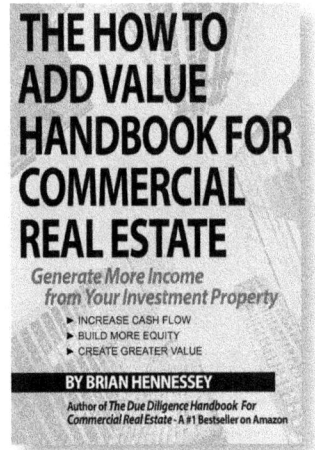

THE HOW TO ADD VALUE HANDBOOK FOR COMMERCIAL REAL ESTATE

Generate More Income from Your Investment Property
- INCREASE CASH FLOW
- BUILD MORE EQUITY
- CREATE GREATER VALUE

BY BRIAN HENNESSEY
Author of The Due Diligence Handbook For Commercial Real Estate - A #1 Bestseller on Amazon

In this handbook you will learn:

- How to determine the best way to price the rental rate for your investment property to get it leased at the highest value
- Find ways to make your property attractive to tenants
- How to interview and choose the right people that will help you get your property leased
- How to structure your lease rate and terms to create the most value for your investment property
- How to incentivize tenants to get your property leased in a down or over crowded market
- Strategies and tips to create more value
- Essential analysis forms, proposal and lease form samples, tenant application and other forms

These are very learnable skills that can be put into use right away to enhance your efforts to add value to your real estate investment. Well worth the time spent learning and implementing them.

I also spent time as a Vice President of Leasing for an investor who owned about 12 million square feet across the U.S, where I had to learn local practices and customs, as well as the ins-and-outs of the various markets such as Los Angeles, Dallas, Houston, Chicago, Orlando and Phoenix. Experiences learned during this phase of my career have also contributed to the contents of this book.

By learning and implementing these essential value-enhancing principles you can easily increase your property's cash flow exponentially. Every day you wait is another day of flushing more money down the drain. Buy it today and start generating more income, instead of hoping it all will work out. You will look back and consider it as one of your best real estate investments. Also available as an audiobook on Audible.com and iTunes.

"Brian Hennessey's books are invaluable staples, for both beginner and veteran alike. In his newest book, Brian again draws on his impressive experience to identify foundational best practices, developed from years in the trenches, and presented in a clear and concise format, creating another must-read, handbook that is, at the same time, both simple and smart."

– Robert McBride, Commercial Real Estate Broker

"This book has a wealth of information that is beneficial for all real estate professionals and owners. We are in the property management business and more and more owners today expect us to operate as asset managers with an eye for creating value for their respective properties. Many of the key elements to creating value through marketing, leasing, tenant mix and the right personnel for each property are included in the book. This is a must read and on-going resource for all who want to make money in the real estate business."

– Jock Ebner, President, Morlin Asset Management, LP

"As a 'value-add' player since the 1970's, I always look for ways to find opportunities in real estate. Whenever lucky enough to find something interesting, then the fun starts. Brian Hennessey's writing can help with that part, both for the seasoned veteran and the novice rookie. He goes into every area I could think of, and even some I have never thought of. A must-read for anyone wanting to make money as a principal real estate player."

– Maury Fagan, Real Estate Investor

"I've been a commercial real estate broker over three decades. After reading *The How to Add Value Handbook for Commercial Real Estate*, I believe it is as valuable as Brian Hennessey's book *The Due Diligence Handbook for Commercial Real Estate*; which I am still referring to so I can be certain that I am not missing anything while conducting due diligence. They contain so much

valuable information, it is practically a "FOUND TREASURE" for anyone involved in commercial real estate, whether a seasoned realtor/broker or an investor/commercial property owner."
    – *Krich Adary, Director, Archetype Commercial Realty*

The *How to Add Value Handbook for Commercial Real Estate* offers an in-the-trenches view of creating value in the real estate market. It's grounded, real world examples underscore the importance of thinking through design and leasing decisions with the end in mind.
    – *William King, AIA Architecture-Planning-Design*

www.ingramcontent.com/pod-product-compliance
Lightning Source LLC
Chambersburg PA
CBHW071200200326
41519CB00018B/5296